THE SOUND OF FLUTES

AND OTHER INDIAN LEGENDS

THE SOUND OF FLUTES
AND OTHER INDIAN LEGENDS

told by Lame Deer, Jenny Leading Cloud,
Leonard Crow Dog, and others

TRANSCRIBED AND EDITED BY
RICHARD ERDOES

PICTURES BY
PAUL GOBLE

PANTHEON BOOKS

To Leonard Crow Dog, Medicine Man at Wounded Knee,
and his father Henry, who told me many of these stories.

Library of Congress Cataloging in Publication Data
Erdoes, Richard. THE SOUND OF FLUTES
SUMMARY: Legends from various North American Plains Indian tribes.
Included are "The Sound of Flutes,"
"The Ghostly Lover," and "The Snake Brothers."
1. Indians of North America—Legends. [1. Indians
of North America—Legends]
I. Goble, Paul. II. Title.
E98.F6E72   398.2   76-8660
ISBN 0-394-83181-0   ISBN 0-394-93181-5 lib. bdg.
Manufactured in the United States of America
10 8 6 4 2 0 1 3 5 7 9

Contents

Introduction

The Sound of Flutes   3
HENRY CROW DOG

Where the Girl Saved Her Brother   10
STRANGE OWL

Iktome, Iktome, Iktome   16
HE DOG

The Dogs Are Having an Election   23
LAME DEER

Spotted Eagle and Black Crow   25
JENNY LEADING CLOUD

Iktome Is Invited for Dinner   31
LEONARD CROW DOG

The Thunderbirds   33
EAGLE ELK

The Snake Brothers   37
LAME DEER

The Shortest Tale Ever Told   44
LAME DEER

Three War Stories   45
JENNY LEADING CLOUD

How the Crow Came To Be Black   57
GOOD WHITE BUFFALO

Iktome and the Hawk   60
JAKE HERMAN

The Vision Quest   63
LAME DEER

Mice Powwow in an Elk Skull   68
STRANGE OWL

The Fastest Animal, the Fastest Man, the Fastest Story 71
LAME DEER

How the Sioux Nation Came into Being 72
LAME DEER

The Coming of Wasicun 74
LEONARD CROW DOG

The Very Angry Ghost 82
SPOTTED ELK

Doing a Trick with Eyeballs 86
RACHEL STRANGE OWL

The Eagle and the Bat 90
LAME DEER

Iktome and the Ducks 91
LAME DEER

The Owl and the Young Warrior 93
HENRY CROW DOG

The Ghostly Lover 95
LAME DEER

The Rabbit Boy 98
JENNY LEADING CLOUD

Tatanka Iyotake's Dancing Horse 103
GEORGE EAGLE ELK

Iyan Hokshi, the Stone Boy 108
HENRY CROW DOG

The White Buffalo Woman 117
LAME DEER

The End of the World 124
JENNY LEADING CLOUD

The Remaking of the World 126
LEONARD CROW DOG

Introduction

This book happened after a lifetime of listening to Indian friends telling the tales and legends of their people—stories told around a fire, drinking thick, black coffee and eating berry soup with fry-bread, or while driving in a car a hundred miles to a tribal pow-wow. The first legend was transcribed in 1952, the last just about a year ago. Not a few of the stories were told to me in my New York apartment when friends from the Dakotas or Montana stopped in for a visit.

About half of the stories are on tapes; others were jotted down as they were told. One or two are written from memory. While listening to some of the tapes, I could hear in the background the song of birds and the hum of insects, even the distant howl of a coyote. Most of those who told the stories were good friends. Some are dead now.

The legends are all Plains Indian tales, mostly Sioux, some Cheyenne, one or two of Gros Ventre or Crow origin. But the Sioux tales outnumber all others, probably because I have so many Sioux friends. In most cases I have several versions of the same story, told by different people. If I say that a tale was told to me by Crow Dog rather than Eagle Elk or Lame Deer, it might be just because of a little personal touch or variation, or perhaps because I can see Crow Dog in my mind telling this particular story, his tall, spare figure silhouetted by the light of an exceptionally beautiful sunset, his arms and hands moving, painting pictures in the air.

Stories are handed on from the older generation to the younger. It is all done by word of mouth—the art is in the telling, the pleasure in listening. Each speaker is an individualist telling the story in his own way. Some legends are sacred, and whoever relates them will make an effort to tell the story just as he heard it from his grandfather, in the same words if possible. Others are fun stories which can be improved upon with each telling. One family tells a legend one way, another family knows it differently. Some stories die because there is nobody left to tell them and nobody to remember. Luckily that does not happen very often.

Sometimes a new story is born and spreads like wildfire, especially if it is a funny one, like the story about an Indian who is invited to lunch by a white friend. The Indian is poor and hungry. "Can I order a steak?" he asks. "Anything you want," says the white friend. The Indian finishes his steak with all the trimmings in record time. But he is still hungry. "Would you treat me to a second steak?" he says. "Sure, go ahead," answers the friend. The second steak arrives and is polished off even faster than the first one. Watching the performance the generous host marvels, "I wish I had your appetite!" "What!" exclaims the Indian. "You guys already took my land, my buffalo, my heritage, my culture, and now you want my appetite, too!"

Tragic or humorous, mystical or heroic, my children and I have enjoyed the tales my Indian friends told me. I hope you will too.

RICHARD ERDOES

THE SOUND OF FLUTES

AND OTHER INDIAN LEGENDS

The Sound of Flutes

Told by Henry Crow Dog

Well, you know our flutes, you have heard their sound and seen how beautifully they are made. That flute of ours, the *Siyotanka*, is a very peculiar instrument. It is made for only one kind of music—love music. In the old days, the young men would sit by themselves, maybe lean against a tree in the dark of the night, hidden, unseen. They would make up their own special tunes, their courting songs.

We Indians have always been shy people. A young man hardly could screw up his courage to talk to a *wincincala*—the pretty girl he was in love with—even if he was a brave warrior who had already counted coup upon an enemy.

There was no privacy in the village, which was only a circle of tipis. No privacy in the family tipi either, which was always crowded with people. And, naturally, you couldn't just walk out into the prairie, hand in hand with your girl, to say sweet words to each other. First, because you didn't hold hands— that would be very unmannerly. You didn't show your af- fection—not by holding hands anyway. Second, you didn't dare

3

take a walk with your wincincala because it wasn't safe. Out there in the tall grass you could be gored by a buffalo, or tomahawked by a Pawnee, or you might run into the U.S. Cavalry.

The only chance you had to meet the one you loved was to wait for her at daybreak when the young girls went to the river or brook with their skin bags to fetch water. Doing that was their job. So, when the girl you had your eye on finally came down the water trail, you popped up from behind some bush, and stood so that she could see you—and that was about all you could do to show her that you were interested—stand there grinning foolishly, looking at your moccasins, scratching your ear, humming a tune.

The wincincala didn't do much either, except get very red in the face, giggle, fiddle with her waterbag, or maybe throw you a wild turnip. The only way she could let you know that she liked you, too, was for her to take a long, long while to do her job, looking back over her shoulder a few times, to peek at you.

So the flutes did all the talking. At night, lying on her buffalo robe in her father's tipi, the girl would hear the soulful, haunting sound of the Siyotanka. She would hear the tune made up especially for her alone, and she would know that out there in the dark a young man was thinking about her.

Well, here I am supposed to relate a legend and instead I am telling you a love story. You see, in all tribes, the flute is used as an expression of a young man's love. It has always been so. And whether it is Sioux, or Pawnee, or Cheyenne, or Shoshone, the flute is always made of cedar wood and shaped like the long neck and the head of a bird with an open beak. The sound comes out of the beak. There is a reason for this, and that's where the legend comes in.

Once, untold generations ago, the people did not know how to make flutes. Drums, rattles, bull-roarers, yes—but no flutes.

In these long-past days, before the white man came with his horse and firestick, a young hunter went out after game. Meat was scarce, and the people in his village were hungry. He found the tracks of an elk and followed them for a long time. The elk is wise and swift. It is the animal that possesses the love-charm. If a man has elk medicine, he will win the one he loves for his wife. He will also be a lucky hunter.

Our poor young man had no elk medicine. After many hours, he finally sighted his game. The young hunter had a fine new bow and a quiver made of otterskin full of good, straight arrows tipped with points of obsidian—sharp, black, and shiny like glass. The young man knew how to use his weapon—he was the best shot in the village—but the elk always managed to stay just out of range, leading the hunter on and on. The young man was so intent on following his prey that he hardly took notice of where he went.

At dusk the hunter found himself deep inside a dense forest of tall trees. The tracks had disappeared, and so had the elk. The young man had to face the fact that he was lost and that it was now too dark to find his way out of the forest. There was not even a moon to show him the way. Luckily, he found a stream with clear, cold water to quench his thirst. Still more luckily, his sister had given him a rawhide bag to take along, filled with *wasna*—pemmican—dried meat pounded together with berries and kidney fat. Sweet, strong wasna—a handful of it will keep a man going for a day or more. After the young man had drunk and eaten, he rolled himself into his fur robe, propped his back against a tree, and tried to get some rest. But he could not sleep. The forest was full of strange noises—the eerie cries of night animals, the hooting of owls, the groaning of trees in the wind. He had heard all these sounds before, but now it seemed as if he were hearing them for the first time. Suddenly there was an entirely new sound, the kind neither he nor any other man had ever experienced before.

It was very mournful, sad, and ghostlike. In a way it made him afraid, so he drew his robe tightly about him and reached for his bow, to make sure that it was properly strung. On the other hand, this new sound was like a song, beautiful beyond imagination, full of love, hope, and yearning. And then, before he knew it, and with the night more than half gone, he was suddenly asleep. He dreamed that a bird called *Wagnuka*, the redheaded woodpecker, appeared to him, singing the strangely beautiful new song, saying, "Follow me and I will teach you."

When the young hunter awoke, the sun was already high, and on a branch of the tree against which he was leaning was a redheaded woodpecker. The bird flew away to another tree and then to another, but never very far, looking all the time over its shoulder at the young man as if to say "Come on!" Then, once more the hunter heard that wonderful song, and his heart yearned to find the singer. The bird flew toward the sound, leading the young man, its flaming red top flitting through the leaves, making it easy to follow. At last the bird alighted on a cedar tree and began tapping and hammering on a dead branch, making a noise like the fast beating of a small drum. Suddenly there was a gust of wind, and again the hunter heard that beautiful sound right close by and above him.

Then he discovered that the song came from the dead branch which the woodpecker was belaboring with its beak. He found,

moreover, that it was the wind which made the sound as it whistled through the holes the bird had drilled into the branch. "*Kola*, friend," said the hunter, "let me take this branch home. You can make yourself another one." He took the branch, a hollow piece of wood about the length of his forearm, and full of holes. The young man walked back to his village. He had no meat to bring to his tribe, but he was happy all the same.

Back in his tipi, he tried to make the dead branch sing for him. He blew on it, he waved it around—but no sound came. It made the young man sad. He wanted so much to hear that wonderful sound. He purified himself in the sweatlodge and climbed to the top of a lonely hill. There, naked, resting with his back against a large rock, he fasted for four days and four nights, crying for a dream, a vision to teach him how to make the branch sing. In the middle of the fourth night, Wagnuka, the bird with the flaming red spot on his head, appeared to him, saying, "Watch me." The bird turned into a man, doing this and that, always saying, "Watch me!" And in his vision the young man watched—very carefully.

When he awoke he found a cedar tree. He broke off a branch, and working many hours hollowed it out delicately with a bowstring drill, just as he had seen Wagnuka do it in his vision. He whittled the branch into a shape of a bird with a long neck and an open beak. He painted the top of the bird's head red with *washasha*, the sacred vermilion color. He prayed. He smoked the branch with incense of burning sage and sweet grass. He fingered the holes as he had watched it done in his dream, all the while blowing softly into the end of his flute. Because this is what he had made—the first flute, the very first *Siyotanka*. And all at once there was the song, ghostlike and beautiful beyond words, and all the people were astounded and joyful.

8

In the village lived an *itancan*, a big and powerful chief. This itancan had a daughter who was beautiful, but also very haughty. Many young men had tried to win her love, but she had turned them all away. Thinking of her, the young man made up a special song, a song that would make this proud wincincala fall in love with him. Standing near a tall tree a little way from the village, he blew his flute.

All at once the wincincala heard it. She was sitting in her father's, the chief's, tipi, feasting on much good meat. She wanted to remain sitting there, but her feet wanted to go outside; and the feet won. Her head said, "Go slow, slow," but her feet said, "Faster, faster." In no time at all she stood next to the young man. Her mind ordered her lips to stay closed, but her heart commanded them to open. Her heart told her tongue to speak.

"*Koshkalaka, washtelake,*" she said. "Young man, I like you." Then she said, "Let your parents send a gift to my father. No matter how small, it will be accepted. Let your father speak for you to my father. Do it soon, right now!"

And so the old folks agreed according to the wishes of their children, and the chief's daughter became the young hunter's wife. All the other young men had heard and seen how it came about. Soon they, too, began to whittle cedar branches into the shapes of birds' heads with long necks and open beaks, and the beautiful haunting sound of flutes traveled from tribe to tribe until it filled the whole prairie. And that is how Siyotanka the flute came to be—thanks to the cedar, the woodpecker, the wind, and one young hunter who shot no elk but who knew how to listen.

9

Where the Girl Saved Her Brother

Told by Strange Owl

Almost exactly a hundred years ago, in the summer of 1876, the two greatest battles between soldiers and Indians were fought on the plains of Montana. The first fight was called the Battle of the Rosebud. The second battle, which was fought a week later, was called the Battle of the Little Big Horn, where General Custer was defeated and killed. The Cheyennes call the Battle of the Rosebud the fight *Where the Girl Saved Her Brother*. Let me tell you why.

But first let me explain what is meant when an Indian says, "I have counted coup." "Counting coup" is gaining war honors. The Indians think that it is easy to kill an enemy by shooting him from ambush. This brings no honor. It is not counting coup. But to ride up to an enemy, or walk up to him while he is still alive, unwounded and armed, and then to hit him with your feathered coup stick, or touch him with your hand, this brings honor and earns you eagle feathers. This is counting coup. To steal horses in a daring raid can also be counting coup. But one of the greatest honors is to be gained by dashing with your horse into the midst of your enemies to rescue a friend, surrounded and unhorsed, to take him up behind you and gallop out again, saving his life by risking your own. That is counting coup indeed, counting big coup.

Well, a hundred years ago, the white men wanted the Indians to go into prisons called "reservations," to give up their freedom to roam and hunt buffalo, to give up being Indians. Some gave in tamely and went to live behind the barbed wire of the agencies, but others did not.

Those who went to the reservations to live like white men were called "friendlies." Those who would not go were called "hostiles." They were not hostile, really. They did not want to fight. All they wanted was to be left alone to live the Indian way, which was a good way. But the soldiers would not let them. They decided to make a great surround and catch all "hostiles," kill those who resisted, and bring the others back as prisoners to the agencies. Three columns of soldiers entered the last stretch of land left to the red man. They were led by Generals Crook, Custer, and Terry. Crook had the most men with him, about two thousand. He also had cannon and Indian scouts to guide him. At the Rosebud he met the united Sioux and Cheyenne warriors.

The Indians had danced the sacred Sun Dance. The great Sioux chief Sitting Bull had been granted a vision telling him

that the soldiers would be defeated. The warriors were in high spirits. Some men belonging to famous warrior societies had vowed to fight until they were killed, singing their death songs, throwing their lives away, as it was called. They painted their faces for war. They put on their finest outfits so that, if they were killed, their enemies should say, "This must have been a great fighter or chief. See how nobly he lies there."

The old chiefs instructed the young men how to act. The medicine men prepared the charms for the fighters, putting gopher dust on their hair, or painting their horses with hailstone designs. This was to render them invisible to their foes, or to make them bulletproof. Brave Wolf had the most admired medicine—a mounted hawk that he fastened to the back of his head. Brave Wolf always rode into battle blowing on his eaglebone whistle—and once the fight started, the hawk came alive and whistled too.

Many proud tribes were there besides the Cheyenne—the Hunkpapa, the Minniconjou, the Oglala, the Burned Thighs, the Two Kettles—and many famous chiefs and brave warriors—Two Moons, White Bull, Dirty Moccasins, Little Hawk, Yellow Eagle, Lame White Man. Among the Sioux was the great Crazy Horse, and Sitting Bull—their holy man, still weak from his flesh offerings made at the Sun Dance—and the fierce Rain-in-the-Face. Who can count them all, and what a fine sight they were!

Those who earned the right to wear war bonnets were singing, lifting them up. Three times they stopped in their singing, and the fourth time they put the bonnets on their heads, letting the streamers fly and trail behind them. How good it must have been to see this! What would I give to have been there!

Crazy Horse of the Oglala shouted his famous war cry, "A

12

good day to die, and a good day to fight. Cowards to the rear, brave hearts—follow me!"

The fight started. Many brave deeds were done, many coups counted. The battle swayed to and fro. More than anybody else's, this was the Cheyenne's fight. This was their day. Among them was a brave young girl, Buffalo Calf Road Woman, who rode proudly at the side of her husband, Black Coyote. Her brother, Chief Comes-in-Sight, was in the battle too. She looked for him and at last saw him. His horse had been killed from under him. He was surrounded. Soldiers were aiming their rifles at him. Their white Crow scouts circled around him, waiting for an opportunity to count cheap coups upon him. But he fought them with bravery and skill.

Buffalo Calf Road Woman uttered a shrill, high-pitched war cry. She raced her pony right into the midst of the battle, into the midst of the enemy. She made the spine-chilling, trilling, warbling sound of the Indian woman encouraging her man during a fight. Chief Comes-in-Sight jumped up on her horse behind his sister. Buffalo Calf Road Woman laughed with joy and with

13

the excitement of battle. Buffalo Calf Road Woman sang while she was doing this. The soldiers were firing at her, and their Crow scouts were shooting arrows at her horse—but it moved too fast for her or Chief Comes-in-Sight to be hit. Then she turned her horse and raced up the hill from which the old chiefs and the medicine men watched the battle. The Sioux and Cheyenne saw what was being done. And then the white soldiers saw it too. They all stopped fighting and just looked at that brave girl saving her brother's life. The warriors raised their arms and set up a mighty shout—a long, trilling, undulating war cry that made one's hairs stand on end. And even some of the soldiers threw their caps in the air and shouted "Hurrah" in honor of Buffalo Calf Road Woman.

The battle was still young. Not many men had been killed on either side, but the white general was thinking, "If their women fight like this, what will their warriors be like? Even if I win, I will lose half my men." And so General Crook retreated a hundred miles or so. He was to have joined up with Custer, Old Yellow Hair, but when Custer had to fight the same Cheyennes and Sioux again a week later, Crook was far away and Custer's army was wiped out. So Buffalo Calf Road Woman in a way contributed to the winning of that famous battle too.

Many who saw what she had done thought that she had counted the biggest coup—not taking life but giving it. That is why the Indians call the Battle of the Rosebud *Where the Girl Saved Her Brother.*

The spot where Buffalo Calf Road Woman counted coup has long since been plowed under. A ranch now covers it. But the memory of her deed lives on—and will live on as long as there are Indians. This is not a fairy tale, but it is a legend.

Iktome, Iktome, Iktome

Told by He Dog

Iktome, the foolish trickster and spider man, was scratching his head because he had lice. His scalp itched. "This is not good," he thought to himself. He saw two *wincincala*, two pretty girls, tanning a hide. He went to them and stretched out, putting his head in the lap of one of them and saying, "Do a good job delousing me." That was not very polite. But the girls took turns combing his hair, killing the lice. It made Iktome drowsy, and he fell asleep. At once the two girls stopped combing him and filled his hair with burrs. When Iktome awoke the girls were gone, but the burrs were there. His hair was full of them. The burrs pulled his hair so that the skin of Iktome's face was drawn tight. He could hardly close his eyes. He had to cut off all his hair in order to get rid of the burrs. He was some sight! Everybody laughed at him, so he decided to go away.

He walked by a stream. Reflected in its water he saw a choke-cherry tree and a bush full of berries. He did not look up to see

16

the tree and the bush. He jumped into the stream to get some berries and chokecherries. He got wet instead.

Iktome went on. He came to a funeral scaffold. On it was the body of a person who had died a long time ago. It smelled very bad. "This body has a terrible odor," said Iktome. The Ghost of the dead man heard him. He came down from the scaffold and grabbed Iktome by the scruff of his neck. "What did you say?" asked the Ghost. "I said that it smelled real good here, like wild roses and sweetgrass." The Ghost let Iktome go, and the frightened spider man ran away as fast as his eight legs could carry him. Yes, eight legs. Most of the time, Iktome goes around looking like a human being, but when he is badly frightened he sometimes turns himself into a spider, at least as far as the legs are concerned.

Iktome went on. He was still out of breath when he came to an old holy man, a medicine man. The old man sang four songs, and when he sang the last one a buffalo came rolling down a cliff, falling dead at his feet. "This is my buffalo song," the old man told Iktome. "It has great power. It keeps me in meat." Iktome started begging, "Please, uncle, teach me this wonderful song." "You look like a selfish, foolish person to me; you do not deserve it," said the old man. "It is not for me," cried Iktome. "Teach me the song for the good of my people who are starving." "In that case I will do it," said the old man, "but you must promise me to use the song only when you and your people are hungry and there is nothing else to eat." Iktome promised. He learned the song. He went on, humming it. A little way off, where the old man could neither see nor hear him, Iktome tried out his new, wonderful song. At once a buffalo came tumbling down a cliff, falling dead at his feet. Iktome took none of the meat. He was not hungry. He had sung the song only for fun. He

17

laughed and went on. Twice more he sang the song to amuse himself and also because it made him feel powerful. Each time, a buffalo crashed down a hillside to fall dead before him. Each time, Iktome laughed and went on. But when he sang the song a fourth time, *the buffalo fell on him!* Iktome lay under the huge beast, crushed and half dead. If coyotes had not come and eaten the buffalo, it would have been the end of Iktome. Thus was he punished for his foolishness.

Iktome went on, limping. He came to a village and entered a tipi from which came the smell of good food. Inside was an old grandmother cooking. It was dark inside the tent. Iktome thought the wrinkled grandmother was a beautiful young girl. He forgot about the food. "Let me kiss you," he asked the old hag. She said, "Why not? *Imaputake.* Kiss me. I am the prettiest girl in the whole village. Iktome embraced the old grandmother. He felt warts and wrinkled skin and a toothless mouth. The old woman cackled. "It is very dark in here," said Iktome. "I will get some light." He went outside and opened his bag, letting the sunshine into it. He closed the bag and carried it inside the tipi. He opened the bag, saying, "Now it will be bright in here." But the tipi was as dark as before. Iktome was disappointed and went away.

Iktome managed to kill some ducks with his bow and arrows.

He made a fire, plucked the ducks, put them on sticks, and began to roast them in the hot, glowing ashes. Just then he saw two trees above him making a noise. The wind had entangled the trees so that bark was rubbing against bark. It sounded like weeping or moaning. "Why are you fighting, you trees?" said the foolish trickster. "Stop it!" But the trees continued rubbing against each other noisily. "I will make peace between you," shouted Iktome. "I will separate you and keep you from fighting." He climbed up between the branches to pull the trees apart. Just then a mighty gush of wind made the trees crash into each other so that Iktome was trapped in the intertwining branches. "Foolish, stupid trees," he shouted. "Let me go!" But he could not free himself.

The delicious smell of roast duck had drawn a coyote to the spot. The coyote is as much of a trickster and pest as Iktome, only he is smarter. The coyote soon was wise to the fact that Iktome was trapped. While Iktome angrily watched, the coyote ate one duck after the other, exclaiming: "Ah, oh, these are the best ducks I ever ate. *Pilamaya*, Iktome, thank you. And thank you once again for inviting me."

At last there was only one duck left, the very best. Iktome had filled it with finely chopped meat and herbs. "Leave me that one, at least," he cried. The coyote stood before the fire so that Iktome could not see what he was doing. He pretended not to hear Iktome. The coyote ate the meat and the herbs inside the duck and filled it with ashes. Then he pushed it back into the smoldering embers. The coyote wiped his mouth with his paw and went away.

Finally, Iktome managed to free himself from the tangled branches. He climbed down and poked around in the fire. He found the duck. "Oh, that fool of a coyote," cried Iktome, "he has overlooked the best one." Iktome bit deep into the roast duck. He came away with a big mouthful of hot ashes. He spit and spit and spit. "I will kill that no-good coyote," he vowed.

Iktome went on following the coyote's tracks. He found his enemy sleeping, snoring. "Now I shall kill and eat him," said Iktome. "Shall I knock him in the head? No, that would spoil the brains, my favorite food. Shall I knock him in the ribs? No, that would spoil the rib meat. Shall I tie a rock to his neck and drown him? No, that would spoil the meat altogether. Besides, how do I get him up from the bottom of the river?" The coyote listened to Iktome talking to himself. He was not asleep at all, only pretending. "I'll lift up that no-good coyote," said Iktome finally, "and throw him in the fire. Coyote barbecue is good. Yes, that's what I'll do." He lifted up the coyote, but before he could throw him into the fire, the coyote jumped out of Iktome's arms, jumped into the river, swam across it, and ran up to the top of a hill on the other side, laughing at Iktome who had stumbled into the flames and burned himself. Angry—and very hungry— Iktome went on his way.

Iktome walked on. He dug up *timpsila*, wild turnips, and ate some. It was better than nothing, but not as good as roast duck. Iktome kept going until he met a giant. The giant was uprooting tall trees—pushing them over, twisting them out of the earth, tearing them loose, roots and all. "*Kanji*, cousin," cried Iktome, "why are you knocking down all the best trees?" "These are good, straight trees," said the giant; "they make good arrows." "Don't you know any better?" asked Iktome. "These are much too big for arrows. You must be *witko*, crazy." "Don't get smart with me," answered the giant, gathering up some tall trees in a bundle. "These are arrow sticks." "In that case," replied Iktome, "show me how you can shoot them. Shoot one at me." "You are

20

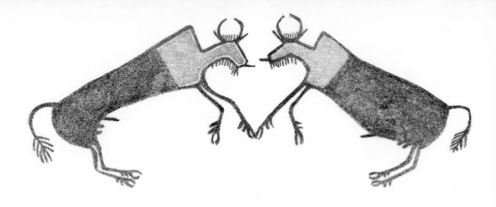

too close," said the giant. Iktome walked a hundred paces. "Still too close," yelled the giant. Iktome went a few hundred steps farther. "Still too close," yelled the giant. Iktome walked a mile. "That's about it," roared the giant and hurled a mighty tree, roots first, at Iktome, not using a bow at all.

The tree floated through the air very slowly, making a noise like thunder. Iktome was afraid. He ran this way and that, trying to dodge that big tree. But the tree followed him wherever he ran. He zigzagged like a rabbit, but the tree zigzagged with him. The frantic Iktome tried to crawl into a rabbit hole in order to escape, but the hole was too small and he could only get his head into it. Then the tree hit him a mighty blow, carrying off his body, leaving only his head sticking in the hole. "Help, help," cried Iktome's head. The giant came over. "What's the matter?" he asked. "*Onshimala ye*," whimpered Iktome. "Have pity. Put me together again." "So sorry," said the giant. "I only wanted to show you how to shoot with trees. Don't worry. I will doctor you." The giant dug Iktome's head out of the hole, smeared some very powerful medicine on the neck, and put it on the body. Iktome was whole again. "What do you think of my arrows?" asked the giant. "In time you could become a good shot," answered Iktome.

Iktome went on, rubbing his neck. He was a little shaken up by all that had happened to him. He got tired and lay down,

21

pulling his buffalo robe over himself. Bad dreams woke him up. In the moonlight he saw two large, ghostly hands reaching out for him from the far end of his buffalo robe. "Ghostly hands, go away," said Iktome, whose hair stood on end. The hands did not go away. "Ghostly hands, go away, or I will have to do something about you." The hands stayed where they were. "Ghostly hands," warned Iktome, "go away or I will get mad." The hands did not budge. "I am telling you for the last time, ghostly hands, go away or I will hit you with my big warclub." Still the hands would not move. Iktome took hold of his warclub, which had a heavy stone head, and struck the ghostly hands with all his might. Iktome yelled with pain, hopping madly from one leg to another, rubbing his bruised toes. Iktome had hit his own feet. "This is not a good place to rest," said Iktome and went on.

Well, Iktome had many more adventures and did a hundred more foolish things. But these are all I remember. Let someone else tell what happened to Iktome later on. What kind of things are still happening to this spider man.

The Dogs Are Having an Election

Told by Lame Deer

You ask me about elections, presidential elections, tribal elections. Well, for twenty-five thousand years we got along without them, as we got along without jails, saloons, banks, insane asylums, courthouses, taxes, lawyers, and telephones. And you white people thought you could improve upon a system like ours. Well, about those elections. The real old-time full bloods won't have anything to do with them. The white government in Washington never did us any good; and as to tribal governments, they are patterned after Washington—white inventions. What have these to do with us, a people who knew how to govern ourselves in a sacred manner for thousands of years without anybody's help? Lice on all politicians, and short arms so that they can't scratch themselves. But, you asked me.

Well, we have a little story, a legend. Once, a long time ago, the dogs were trying to elect a president. So one of them got up in that big Dog Convention and said, "I propose the bulldog for president. He is strong, he can fight."

"But he can't run," said another dog. "What good is it that he can fight if he can't run? He won't catch anybody."

Then another dog got up and said, "I propose the greyhound for president. He sure can run."

But all the other dogs cried, "Naw, he can run all right, but he can't fight. When he catches up with somebody, what happens then? He gets the hell beaten out of him, that's what."

Then an ugly little mutt of a dog jumped up and said, "I propose that dog for president who smells good underneath its tail."

And immediately an equally ugly mutt jumped up and yelled, "I second the motion."

All at once, all the dogs started sniffing underneath each other's tails, and a big chorus went up among the dogs: "Phew, he doesn't smell good," "No, neither this one," and, "He's no presidential timber either," and, "No, him no good either," and, "This one sure is not the people's choice," and, "Wow, this sure ain't my candidate."

Now if you go out for a walk, just watch the dogs. They are still looking for a good leader. They still haven't found him.

Spotted Eagle and Black Crow

Told by Jenny Leading Cloud

This is a story of two warriors, of jealousy, and of eagles. This legend is supposed to have been a favorite of the great *Mahpiya Luta*—Chief Red Cloud of the Oglalas.

Many lifetimes ago, there lived two brave warriors. One was named *Wanblee Gleska*—Spotted Eagle. The other's name was *Kangi Sapa*—Black Crow. They were friends but, as it happened, they both loved the same girl, *Zintkala Luta Win*—Red Bird. She was beautiful, a fine tanner and quill-worker, and she liked Spotted Eagle best, which made Black Crow very jealous.

Black Crow went to his friend and said, "Let us, you and I, go on a war party against the Pahani. Let us get ourselves some fine horses and earn eagle feathers." Spotted Eagle thought this a good idea. The two young men purified themselves in a sweat bath. They got out their war medicine and their war shields. They painted their faces. They did all that warriors should do before a raid. Then they went against the Pahani.

Their raid was not a success. The Pahani were watchful. The

25

young warriors got nowhere near the Pahani horse herd. Not only did they capture no ponies, but they even lost their own mounts, because while they were trying to creep up to their enemies' herd, the Pahani found their horses. The two young men had a hard time getting away on foot because the enemy were searching for them everywhere. At one time they had to hide themselves in a lake, under the water, breathing through long, hollow reeds which were sticking up above the surface. They were so clever at hiding themselves that the Pahani finally gave up searching for them.

The young men had to travel home on foot. It was a long way. Their moccasins were tattered, their feet bleeding. At last they came to a high cliff. "Let us go up there," said Black Crow, "and see whether the enemy is following us." They climbed up. They could see no one following them; but on a ledge far below them, halfway up the cliff, they spied a nest with two young eagles in it. "Let us at least get those eagles," Black Crow proposed. There was no way one could climb down the sheer rock wall, but Black Crow took his rawhide lariat, made a loop in it, put the rope around Spotted Eagle's chest under his armpits, and lowered him down. When his friend was on the ledge with the nest, Black Crow said to himself, "I will leave him there to die. I will come home alone and then Red Bird will marry me." And he threw his end of the rawhide thong down and left without looking back and without listening to Spotted Eagle's cries of what had happened to the lariat and to Black Crow.

Spotted Eagle cried in vain. He got no answer, only silence. At last it dawned on him that his companion had betrayed him, that he had been left to die. The lariat was much too short for him to lower himself to the ground; there was an abyss of two hundred feet yawning beneath him. He was left with the two

young eagles screeching at him, angered that this strange, two-legged creature had invaded their home.

Black Crow came back to his village. "Spotted Eagle died a warrior's death," he told the people. "The Pahani killed him." There was loud wailing throughout the village because everybody had liked Spotted Eagle. Red Bird grieved more than the others. She slashed her arms with a sharp knife and cut her hair to make plain her sorrow to all. But in the end she became Black Crow's wife, because life must go on.

But Spotted Eagle did not die on his lonely ledge. The eagles got used to him. The old eagles brought plenty of food—rabbits, prairie dogs, or sage hens—and Spotted Eagle shared this raw meat with the two chicks. Maybe it was the eagle medicine in his bundle which he carried on his chest that made the eagles accept him. Still, he had a very hard time on that ledge. It was so narrow that, when he wanted to rest, he had to tie himself with the rawhide thong to a little rock sticking out of the cliff, for fear of falling off the ledge in his sleep. In this way he spent a few very uncomfortable weeks; after all, he was a human being and not a bird to whom such a crack in the rock face is home.

At last the young eagles were big enough to practice flying. "What will become of me now?" thought the young warrior. "Once these fledglings have flown the nest for good, the old birds won't be bringing any more food up here." Then he had an inspiration. "Perhaps I will die. Very likely I will die. But I will try it. I will not just sit here and give up." He took his little pipe out of the medicine bundle and lifted it to the sky and prayed, "*Wakan Tanka, onshimala ye.* Great Spirit, pity me. You have created man and his cousin, the eagle. You have given me the eagle's name. I have decided to try to let the eagles carry me to the ground. Let the eagles help me, let me succeed."

He smoked and felt a surge of confidence. He grabbed hold of the legs of the two young eagles. "Brothers," he told them, "you have accepted me as one of your own. Now we will live together, or die together. *Hokahay*." And he jumped off the ledge. He expected to be shattered on the ground below, but with a mighty flapping of wings the two young eagles broke his fall and all landed safely. Spotted Eagle said a prayer of thanks to the Ones Above. He thanked the eagles, telling them that one day he would be back with gifts and have a giveaway in their honor.

Spotted Eagle returned to his village. The excitement was great. He had been dead and had come back to life. Everybody asked him how it happened that he was not dead, but he would not tell them. "I escaped," he said, "and that is all." He saw his love married to his treacherous friend, but bore it in silence. He was not one to bring enmity to his people, to set one family against the other. Besides, what happened could not be changed. Thus he accepted his fate.

A year or so later, a great war party of Pahani attacked his village. The enemy outnumbered them tenfold, and there was no chance of victory for Spotted Eagle's band. All the warriors could do was to fight a slow rear-guard action, which would give the helpless ones—the women, children, and old folks—a chance to escape across the river. Guarding their people this way, the few warriors at hand fought bravely, charging the enemy again and again, making them halt and regroup. Each time, the warriors retreated a little, taking up a new position on a hill, or across a gully. In this way they could save their families.

Showing the greatest courage, exposing their bodies freely,

were Spotted Eagle and Black Crow. In the end they alone faced the enemy. Then, suddenly, Black Crow's horse was hit by several arrows in succession and collapsed under him. "Brother, forgive me for what I have done," he cried to Spotted Eagle. "Let me jump up on your horse behind you."

Spotted Eagle answered, "You are a Fox. Pin yourself and fight. Then, if you survive, I will forgive you; and if you die, I will forgive you also."

What Spotted Eagle meant was this: Black Crow was a member of the Fox Warrior Society. The braves who belong to it sing this song:

> *I am a Fox.*
> *If there is anything daring,*
> *If there is anything dangerous to do,*
> *That is a task for me to perform.*
> *Let it be done by me.*

Foxes wear a long, trailing sash, decorated with quillwork, which reaches all the way to the ground even when the warrior is on horseback. In the midst of battle, a Fox will sometimes defy death by pinning his sash to the earth with a special wooden pin, or with a knife or arrow. This means: I will stay here, rooted to this spot, facing my foes, until someone comes to release the pin, or until the enemies flee, or until I die.

Black Crow pinned his sash to the ground. There was no one to release him, and the enemy did not flee. Black Crow sang his death song. He was hit by lances and arrows and died a warrior's death. Many Pahani died with him.

Spotted Eagle had been the only one to see this. He finally joined his people, safe across the river. The Pahani had lost all taste to follow them there. "Your husband died well," Spotted

29

Eagle told Red Bird. After some time had passed, Spotted Eagle married Red Bird. And much, much later he told his parents, and no one else, how Black Crow had betrayed him. "I forgive him now," he said, "because once he was my friend, and because he died like a warrior should, fighting for his people, and also because Red Bird and I are happy now."

After a long winter, when spring came again, Spotted Eagle told his wife, " I must go away for a few days to fulfill a promise. I must go alone." He rode off by himself to that cliff. Again he stood at its foot, below the ledge where the eagles' nest had been. He pointed his sacred pipe to the four directions, down to Grandmother Earth and up to the Grandfather, letting the smoke ascend to the sky, calling out: "*Wanblee, misunkala.* Little eagle brothers, hear me."

High above him in the clouds appeared two black dots, circling. These were the eagles who had saved his life. They came at his call, their huge wings spread majestically, uttering a shrill cry of joy and recognition. Swooping down, they alighted at his feet. He stroked them with a feather fan, and thanked them many times, and fed them choice morsels of buffalo meat, and fastened small medicine bundles around their legs as a sign of friendship, and spread sacred tobacco offerings around the foot of the cliff. Thus he made a pact of friendship and brotherhood between *Wanblee Oyate*—the Eagle Nation—and his own people. After he had done all this, the stately birds soared up again into the sky, circling motionless, carried by the wind, disappearing into the clouds. Spotted Eagle turned his horse's head homeward, going happily back to Red Bird.

Iktome Is Invited for Dinner

Told by Leonard Crow Dog

Iktome, the spider man and prankster, was invited by a friend to visit him in his tipi and eat there. Now this friend belonged to a different tribe. Iktome did not know the customs of those people, or the kind of food they ate.

Iktome's friend brought two fine, big, young buffalo-bull livers to his wife and said, "Please cook these for myself and for my friend Iktome." Then he went out on an errand. The wife put the livers on a stick and began to roast them over her cooking fire. How good they smelled. Buffalo liver was her favorite food. "I'll take just one small bite," she said to herself; "nobody will miss it." But after she had taken that first bite, she couldn't stop. Well, she ate one liver and still was not satisfied. So she ate the other liver as well. "What will I do now?" she thought. "My husband will beat me." Just then Iktome came into the tipi. "It's about eating time," he said, "and I am hungry, but I see no meat cooking."

"Well, you are a stranger here," said the wife, "and you don't know our ways. What we like best is human ears roasted brown and crisp. Human ears, that's what we are having tonight."

"Human ears," cried Iktome. "Whose human ears?"

"Yours," said the woman, sharpening her skinning knife.

"Not mine," cried Iktome, running away as if a horde of wolves were after him.

Just then the husband came home and saw Iktome running away. "What's the matter with him?" he asked his wife.

"A fine friend you have invited," the woman told him. "How greedy he is. Not satisfied with his share, he took both livers and made off with them."

The man ran after Iktome. "Leave me one at least," he cried, "only one."

"If you catch me, you can have both of them," Iktome yelled back at him.

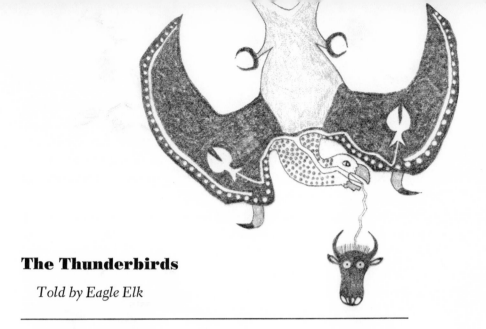

The Thunderbirds

Told by Eagle Elk

This is the *ohunkakan,* or legend, of the Thunderbirds, the mightiest creatures in the universe. When the earth was young, the Thunderbirds had no wings. As a matter of fact, they were not birds at all then, but giants. They ruled over the waters. They dug out huge ditches for riverbeds so that the big and little streams could flow in them. They dug deep holes which became lakes. They fought the Great Water Monster, which was covered all over with red hair. The monster had a single huge eye and a long, curved horn in the center of its forehead. Its arched back-bone was as big as a mountain. Those who saw it went blind on the first day. On the second day they became mad, and on the third day they died. The Great Water Monster was indeed a frightful creature, and it was the giants who challenged it to battle and finally killed it. The monster's huge, petrified bones are still strewn all through the badlands, the moon landscapes of twisted erosions that dot the western plains. The scientists of to-day say that these are dinosaur bones. Let them. In the badlands, too, you can find the *kangi tamé*—bolts of lightning hurled by the Thunderbirds, which look like black stones and are shaped like spearpoints.

The giants lived ten times longer than ordinary human beings. In the end, though, they died like all living things. Only the mountains and the sun last forever. The giants' spirits went up into the sky, high above the clouds, turning into *Wakinyan*—Thunderbirds. Their earthly bodies turned into stones like those of the bones of the Great Water Monster. Way beyond the clouds, at the world's end, where the sun goes down, is the mountain where the Wakinyan dwell. Some say that a few of the younger Thunderbirds used to dwell in the *Paha Sapa*, the Sacred Black Hills, given to the Indians for "as long as the sun shall shine, and as long as the grass shall grow," but stolen from them as soon as gold was found there. But we have not given up trying to get these holy mountains back, desecrated as they are now with cheap tourist attractions. Once the Paha Sapa are Indian Land again, maybe the Thunderbirds will come back too? But I am straying from my story.

As I said, the Thunderbirds have their mountain home way, way above the plains; but they can make themselves invisible to human eyes, especially white eyes. We know about them mostly from dreams. Many Indians have seen them in their visions. Four paths lead into the Thunderbirds' mountain. A butterfly guards the entrance to the East, a bear guards the West, a deer the North, and a beaver to the South. The Thunderbirds have a gigantic nest made of dry bones, the Water Monster's leftover bones. In it rests the great egg from which the Thunderbirds are

hatched. The egg is huge beyond imagination, bigger than all of South Dakota.

There are four large, old Thunderbirds. The Great Wakinyan of the West is the first and foremost among them. He is clothed in clouds. His body is formless, but he has giant, four-jointed wings. He has no feet, but enormous claws. He has no head, but a huge sharp beak with rows of equally sharp teeth. His color is black. The second Thunderbird is red. The third Thunderbird is yellow. The fourth Thunderbird is blue—he has neither eyes nor ears.

It is not easy to describe a Thunderbird—a face without features, a shape without form, claws without feet, a beak without a head. From time to time, a holy man catches a glimpse of a Wakinyan in his dreams, but always only a part of him. No one ever sees a Thunderbird whole, not even in a vision. If this story ever gets into a book, I pity the artist who has to illustrate this. He will have a problem. I hope he will take a sweat bath and go on a vision quest, fasting for four days and nights on a lonely hilltop. Maybe then he will see the Thunderbird in his mind. If he is lucky.

The Thunderbirds are part of the *Wakan Oyate*, the world of the supernaturals. You can call them gods. When they open their beaks they talk thunder, and all the little Thunderbirds repeat after them. That is why you hear a great thunderclap first, and smaller rumblings later. Every time the Wakinyan open their eyes, lightning shoots out of them, even in the case of the Wakinyan with no eyes. He has half moons instead of eyes, but his lightning is just as fierce as that of the others.

The Thunderbirds are about the most powerful beings in the universe. You could say they have atomic power, power given to them by *Wi*, the sun, and also power of fire and water, the good power of light, and the power of killing—good and bad power, as everything in nature has its good and its bad side, at least from the human point of view. But what do human beings know about the universe's big plan? Not very much.

The old people used to say that all the damage caused by lightning is caused by young, inexperienced Thunderbirds who do not yet know how to control it. The wise, old Thunderbirds never kill anyone. Well, that at least is the story. If you tell a tale and someone thinks that you are not telling the truth, then you swear by the Thunderbirds that you did not lie, and everybody knows then that you have told nothing but the truth. Otherwise, lightning would strike you dead.

One thing more. If you happen to dream about the Wakinyan, that will make you into a *heyoka*, a clown, a forward-backward, yes-and-no man. A heyoka says "I hate you" when he wants to say "I love you." When he feels like laughing, he cries. When it is very hot, his teeth chatter, and he covers himself with furs. When it is cold, he walks around naked, with only a loincloth on; and he always sits his horse backward. Now, if you get tired of being a heyoka, there is only one thing you can do to become normal again. You must undergo a ceremony in the course of which you have to plunge your bare arm into a boiling kettle of dog meat. So you had better think twice before dreaming about Thunderbirds.

The Snake Brothers

Told by Lame Deer

For a long time people have been saying that somewhere near Soldiers Creek a giant rattlesnake has its den. It is supposed to be a full twelve feet long and very old. Nobody has seen it for many years now, but there are people who say that they have smelled it and heard its many huge, vibrating rattles as they passed by the spot where the big snake is supposed to live.

Rattlers are funny critters. Their eyesight is poor, but on each side of their faces they have a small hole, and through this hole they can sense the heat of a warm-blooded animal and strike even when it is dark. Rattlers are perfect gentlemen. They will let you know that they are around by rattling their tails, which is their way of saying, "Cousin, please leave me alone, and I will leave you alone, too."

For some reason, there used to be a lot of rattlesnakes on the Rosebud Rodeo Grounds. In some years one had to clear them out of that place so that they wouldn't frighten the white folks who came to see the bronc busting. Anyhow, all this talk about snakes is my way of leading up to another old legend, the tale of the Snake Brothers.

A long time ago, when the earth was young, there were four brothers, all of them young and skilled at hunting, who went out scouting for buffalo. It was not long before they saw a lone buffalo. They killed him with their arrows. All at once they heard a voice, the voice of a buffalo speaking human words. "Take the meat to nourish yourselves; but put the skin, head, hooves, and tail together, every part in its place. Do this for sure."

The youngest of the brothers said, "Let us do as the voice told us, let us do it together." But the other three young men did not want to bother. "That was a foolish voice," they said, "maybe no voice at all. We only imagined hearing it. We will take the skin home to the village. It will make a fine winter robe." The youngest brother had to argue long and hard, and finally take the skin, offering to fight them for it, before they would do what the voice had told them.

While the other three feasted on buffalo hump and lay down to get some rest, the youngest brother went to the top of a hill and spread out the skin, and skull, and bones—just as the voice

had told him. He said a prayer to the buffalo, who gave of his flesh so that the people should live. And as he prayed, right before his eyes, all the various parts of the buffalo joined themselves together and came alive again, forming themselves into a whole animal once more, into a fine, strong buffalo who bellowed loudly and then walked slowly off to disappear beyond the hills. The youngest brother watched the buffalo as long as his eyes could follow it. Only when he could no longer see it did he join the others around the fire.

He ate some of what the others had left for him. They had taken the best parts. They made fun of him for having missed the best tidbits. They said, "We will still go and take the skin, whether you like it or not." But the skin was gone, together with all the other parts. The youngest brother told them what had happened, but they would not believe him. "You are trying to fool us," they said. "You have buried everything somewhere."

After that, all four brothers stretched out to sleep. In the middle of the night the oldest brother woke up, saying, "What is this noise I hear every time I move in my sleep?" The noise was a rattling sound, and it came from his feet. He looked down. In the dim light of the dying fire he saw that his feet had grown rattles. He called out to the others, "Come over here, something strange has happened to my feet."

But only the youngest brother came to look. The others would have come, but they could not. "There is something the matter with my legs, too," cried the second oldest brother. He found that his feet had become stuck together so that he could not get them apart. "And look at my legs," cried the third oldest. His legs were not only stuck together, but rounded, looking like a snake's tail. "I think we are being punished," said the oldest

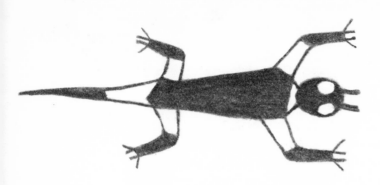

brother, "for not having obeyed that voice." While they were debating this, the change moved up to their hips. "Now I know we are being punished," said the second oldest brother. "We are being turned into snakes." "My body is already covered with scales," cried the third oldest brother. By then, the change had moved up to their necks.

"Do not worry, *misunkala*, younger brother," said the older ones. "Though we are going to be snakes, we will still remain your brothers. We will still look after our village and our people. You see this hill, it has a big hole. This is the entrance to the home of the snakes. We will go in there. Whenever you need help, go there and call us. Come to see us in a little while. At first, come here alone. The second time, bring the people. It is time for us to leave you." More than this they could not say because their heads had been changed into snakes' heads. Now they could only hiss.

"Elder brothers," said the youngest one, weeping, "it was your fate to become snakes. I believe this was to happen to you, that the Great Spirit planned it this way. I will come back as you have told me to do, first alone and then with our people. Farewell."

He saw that his snake brothers had trouble crawling in a snake way. They had still to learn how. So he carried them to the hole in the hillside one by one. They were big snakes, as big and heavy as people. Once he had carried them to the entrance of their snake home, they began to wiggle. They managed to crawl in, one after the other. The youngest brother saw them disappear. For a while he heard them rattle inside. The sound of their rattles grew fainter and fainter—then it stopped. His older brothers had vanished inside. He was alone. He dried his tears and gathered up the buffalo meat to bring to his people. After all, that was what he had come to do.

When he reached the lodges of his people, he told them, "You see I have come back alone. My three older brothers are gone. Do not mourn for them. They are still alive, having been turned into snakes. They now dwell in the hill which is the snakes' home. There you will meet them someday. It was fated to be so."

Four times four days later, the youngest brother prepared to go with a war party against the Pahani on a horse-stealing raid. He painted his face for war. He took his best pony and rode out to the hill where he had left his brothers. He went to the hole at the foot of the hill and called out, "Elder brothers, I have come as you have told me. I have come alone. I need your help."

At once the big head of a giant snake thrust itself through the hole. Its tongue flickered in and out as in greeting. He knew this to be his eldest brother. Then two more big snakes' heads appeared, and he knew that these were his second and third eldest

brothers. They crawled up to him, puting their heads on his arms and shoulders. They hissed at him, and he knew it was their way of wishing him a good day. They looked at him with yellow eyes.

"Brothers, I need your help," he said. "I am going to count coup upon the Pahani."

Many more snakes came out of the hole, setting up a mighty rattling which made the ground tremble. One of the big snakes, the oldest brother, went back into the hole. It reappeared soon, pushing a medicine bundle toward him.

"Eldest brother," said the youngest one, "I know that you are giving me snake medicine. It will give me speed and enable me to wiggle out of any bad situation. It will make me feared by the enemy. It will cause me to strike swiftly with a deadly weapon. Thank you, brothers."

It was as he had said. He struck quickly with the speed of a rattlesnake. His enemy was afraid of him. He counted many coups on them and returned unharmed with many Pahani horses. The people were happy over it. He told them, "Now we must give thanks to my elder brothers."

All the people went with him, and he led them to the hill which was the snakes' home. There he called out for his elder brothers to show themselves. His brothers quickly appeared with much hissing and rattling. The people made offerings to them of tobacco and good, red meat, and the snake brothers were well contented. From then on, they protected the people with powerful snake medicine every time they had to go to war. And from then on, the people were always successful in their enterprises. If the big, human rattlesnakes have not died in the meantime, they are still helping the tribe with their powerful medicine today.

The Shortest Tale Ever Told

Told by Lame Deer

Grandmother Left Hand Bull was telling the story of the frog and the turtle. "And I will bet you," she said, "that this is the shortest legend ever told."

Keha, the turtle, and Gnaske, the frog, were old friends. One day the frog and the turtle were sitting on a rock by the lake gossiping. Suddenly a storm came up, and a few raindrops fell. The turtle looked up anxiously to the sky, saying, "I don't want to get wet, that would give me the sniffles."

"You are right," said the frog, "it wouldn't do to get wet. "Let's hurry!" And with that, they both jumped into the lake. There! . . .

Three War Stories

Told by Jenny Leading Cloud

Nebraska, for the most part, is green and flat. It is part of the great corn belt. There are farms everywhere, and silos. Most of it does not look like the West at all. But as you travel on toward the setting sun, you come to three great rocks which rise out of the plains. First you see one rock, then two others that are like twins. The first one is Chimney Rock. It rises like a needle from the prairie. It was a famous landmark for settlers who traveled west on the Oregon Trail, or to the goldfields of Colorado in their lumbering covered wagons. Then come the twins—Courthouse Rock and Jailhouse Rock. They are of yellowish stone. They are covered with yucca plants and sage brush. Mudswallows nest in the rock faces. One can climb these twin rocks and have a wonderful view of the plains all around. Beyond the rocks rise the chalk cliffs and the sandhills of Nebraska, home of many western Sioux. About Courthouse Rock there is a story.

A long time ago, a war party of our people, the Lakota, surprised a war party of Pahani near Courthouse Rock. We Sioux had been fighting many battles with the Pahani. All these wars

45

between Indian tribes were really the fault of the whites because they pushed nations that had dwelled farther east, in the land of the Great Lakes, beyond the Mississippi and Missouri rivers, into the prairie and into the hunting grounds of other tribes. This, at any rate, happened to us and to the Cheyenne. Maybe the Pahani were there before us. Who knows? At any rate, we were hunting the same buffalo herds in the same place, so naturally we fought.

I guess there must have been more of us than of the Pahani. They retreated to the top of Courthouse Rock to save themselves from an enemy that outnumbered them. Now three sides of Courthouse Rock go straight up and down, like the sides of a skyscraper. No one can climb them. Only the fourth side has a path to the top. It can be easily defended by a few brave men.

The Pahani were on the top and the Sioux at the foot of Courthouse Rock. The chief who led the Sioux told his warriors, "It is no use trying to storm this rock. Women and children could defend it easily. All the advantage is with those on top. Only three or four men abreast can go up that path. But they have no water up there and will soon run out of food. They can stay up there and starve to death, or die of thirst, or come down and fight us on the plain. If they do that, we will defeat them, kill them, and count many coups upon them." The warriors thought that their chief had spoken wisely. The Sioux settled down at the foot of the rock and waited.

On the summit, the Pahani suffered from hunger and thirst. They felt weak. There was little hope for them. But they had a

brave leader who knew how to use his head. He knew, of course, that the Sioux guarded the only path leading down. Three sides of the rock were unguarded, but one had to be a bird to climb down them. On one of these three steep sides, however, there was a round bulge jutting out from the rock face. "If we could fasten a rope to it, we could let ourselves down," thought the Pahani leader. But the outcropping was too smooth, round, and wide to fasten a lasso onto it. The Pahani leader then tried his knife on the rock. The stone was soft, and the knife bit into it easily. The Pahani patiently began to whittle a groove around this bulge. They worked only at night, so that the Sioux would not see what they were up to.

After two nights, they had finished the work. They then tied all their ropes of rawhide together, making one big rope, and found that it reached to the ground. The third night, the Pahani leader tied one end of his long rope to the bulge in the rock by means of the groove. He himself tested it, climbing down and then climbing up again. This took him most of the night. When it grew dark for the fourth time, he told his men, "Now we do it. Let the youngest warrior go first." The Pahani climbed down one by one, the youngest and least accomplished first, the elder and more experienced warriors later. The leader came down last. The Sioux did not notice them, and all got away safely.

The Sioux stayed at the foot of the rock many days. They became hungry because they had hunted out all the game. At last a young warrior said, "They must be all dead up there. I am fed up waiting. I will go up and see." He climbed the path to the top. He called out to those below, "There is nobody up here."

That time the joke was on us Sioux. It is always good telling a story honoring a brave enemy, especially when the story is true.

The Lakota and the *Shahiyela,* the Cheyennes, have been good friends for a long time. Many times they have fought shoulder to shoulder together. They fought the white soldiers on the Bozeman Road, which we Indians called the Thieves' Road because it was built to steal our land. They fought together on the Rosebud, and the two tribes united to defeat Custer in the Battle of the Little Big Horn. Even now, in a barroom brawl, a Sioux will always come to the aid of a Cheyenne, and in any kind of dispute a Cheyenne will side with a Sioux. We Sioux will never forget what brave fighters the Cheyenne used to be.

Over a hundred year ago, the Cheyenne had a famous war chief. The whites called him Roman Nose. He had the fierce, proud face of a hawk. His many deeds were legendary. He always rode into battle with his long war bonnet trailing behind him. Each of its many eagle feathers denoted a brave deed, a coup counted on the enemy.

Roman Nose had a powerful war medicine. It was a magic stone he carried tied to the hair on the back of his head. He always sprinkled his war shirt with sacred gopher dust before a fight and painted his horse with hailstone patterns. All these things, especially the stone, made him bulletproof. Of course he could be slain by a lance, a knife, or a tomahawk; but nobody ever got the better of Roman Nose in hand-to-hand combat. There was, however, something peculiar about Roman Nose's medicine—he was not allowed to touch anything made of metal when eating. He had to eat with horn or wooden spoons, and from wooden or earthenware bowls. His meat had to be cooked in a buffalo's pouch or in a clay pot, not in a white man's iron kettle.

Once he received a message that there was a big fight between white soldiers and Indians. The fight had been swaying back and forth for over a day. "Come and help us, we need you." That was the message. Roman Nose called his warriors together. They ate in a hurry. Roman Nose forgot about the rules he had to live by. He ate buffalo meat cooked in an iron kettle. He ate it with a metal spoon and cut it with a white man's steel knife.

The white soldiers had forted up on an island in the middle of a river, on a sandspit. They had made themselves a barricade of cotton wood tree trunks. They were shooting from behind these fallen trees with a new type of rifle that could shoot faster and farther than the Indians' arrows and old muzzle loaders.

The Cheyenne were hurling themselves against the soldiers in attack after attack; but the water in some spots came up to the saddles of their horses, and the river bottom was slippery. They could not get at the whites as fast as they would have liked, and they had to ride in the face of a murderous fire. The attacks were therefore all repulsed with heavy losses. Roman Nose got ready for the fight. He put on his finest clothes, war shirt, and leggings. He prepared his finest horse, painting him with hailstone designs. He put the pebble in his hair at the back of his head, the pebble that made him bulletproof. At that moment an old warrior stepped up to him, "This sacred stone will do you no good today.

49

Your medicine is bad for this fight. You have eaten from an iron kettle, eaten with a metal spoon, cut your meat with a steel knife. This has rendered your medicine powerless. You must not fight today. You must purify yourself for four days. Only after that will your medicine be good again."

"I know this," said Roman Nose, "but the fight is today, not four days from now. I must lead my warriors. I will die, but only the mountains and the rocks are forever." Roman Nose put on his great war bonnet. He sang his death song and then he charged. He rode up to the breastwork of the soldiers when the bullet hit him in the chest. He fell from his horse, and his body was immediately rescued by his warriors. Then the Cheyenne retreated with the body of their dead chief. To honor him in death, to give him a fitting burial, was more important than to continue the battle. All night through, the soldiers could hear the mourning songs in the Indian camp, the keening of the women. They, too, knew that the great chief Roman Nose was dead. He had died as he had lived. He had shown that sometimes it is more important to act like a chief than to live to a great old age.

Over a hundred years ago, when many Sioux were still living in what is now Minnesota, there dwelled at Spirit Lake a band of Hunkpapa Sioux under a chief called *Tawa Makoce*, His Country. It *was* his country, too, Indian country until the white soldiers with their cannon finally drove the Lakota tribes across the *Mni Shoshay*, the Big Muddy, the Missouri.

In his youth the chief had been one of the greatest warriors. In his later years, when his fighting days were over, he was known

as a wise leader, invaluable in council, and as a great giver of feasts, a provider for the poor. The chief had three sons and one daughter. The sons tried to be warriors as great as their father, but that was a hard thing to do. Again and again they battled the Crow Indians with reckless bravery, exposing themselves in the front rank, fighting hand to hand, until, one by one, they were all killed. Now only his daughter was left to the sad old chief. Her name was Makahta. Others say that she was called *Winyan Ohitika*, Brave Woman.

The girl was beautiful and proud, and many a young man sent his father to the old chief to speak for him, asking Brave Woman as a wife for his son. They brought many fine horses as gifts to back them up. Among those who desired her as a wife was a young warrior named Red Horn, himself the son of a chief, who sent his father again and again to win her for him. But Brave Woman would not marry. "I will not take a husband," she said, "unless I have ridden against the Crow and counted coup on them, avenging my dead brothers." There was another young man who loved Brave Woman. His name was *Wanblee Cikala*, or Little Eagle. He was too shy to make his love known because he was a poor, no-account boy who had never been able to distinguish himself.

At this time the *Kangi Oyate*, the Crow Nation, made a great effort to establish themselves along the banks of the upper Missouri in country that the Sioux considered their own. It was therefore determined to send out a strong war party to chase them back. Among the young warriors riding out against the Crow were Red Horn and Little Eagle. Brave Woman said, "I shall ride with you." She put on her best white buckskin dress richly decorated with beads and porcupine quills. Around her neck she wore a choker of dentalium shells. She took her brothers' weapons and her father's best war pony. She went to the old chief. "Father," she said, "I must go where my brothers died. I must count coup for them. I cannot stay behind. Tell me I may go."

The old chief wept with pride and sorrow. "You are my last child," he answered her, "and I fear for you and for a lonely old age without children to comfort me. But your mind has long been made up in this matter. You are my daughter, your brave brothers' sister. I see that you must go. Do it quickly. I cannot hold back my tears. Take my war bonnet into battle. Go. Do not look back."

And so his daughter rode with the warriors. They found a huge enemy village. It seemed that the whole Crow Nation was there—hundreds of men and thousands of horses. There were many more Crow than Sioux; nevertheless, the Sioux attacked. Brave Woman was a sight to stir the warriors to great deeds. To Red Horn she gave her oldest brother's lance and shield. "Count coup for my dead brother," she said. To Little Eagle she gave her second oldest brother's bow and arrows. "Count coup for him who owned these," she told him. To another young warrior she gave her youngest brother's warclub. She herself carried only her father's old, curved coup stick, wrapped in otter fur.

At first, Brave Woman held back from the fight, encouraging the warriors by singing brave songs and by making the shrill, trembling war cry with which Indian women encourage their men. But when the Sioux, her own warriors from the Hunkpapa

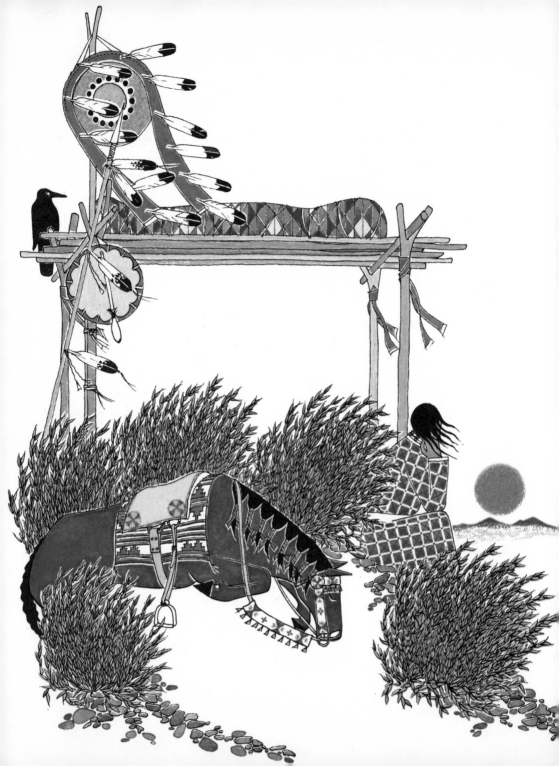

band, were driven back by overwhelming numbers, she herself rode into the midst of the battle. She did not try to kill her enemies, but counted coup left and right, touching them with her coup stick. With a woman fighting so bravely among them, what Sioux warrior could think of retreat? Still, the press of the many Crow and their horses drove them back a second time. Brave Woman's horse was hit by a musket bullet and went down. She was on foot, defenseless. Red Horn passed her on his speckled pony. She was too proud to call out to him for help. He pretended not to see her. Then Little Eagle came riding toward her out of the dust of battle. He at once dismounted, telling her to get on his horse. She did so expecting him to get up behind her. But he would not do so.

"This horse is wounded," he said. "It is too weak to carry us both."

"I will not leave you, then," she told him. "You are sure to be killed."

He took the bow, her brother's bow, and struck the horse sharply with it across the rump. The horse bolted. That was what he had wanted. He went back into the dust of battle—on foot. Brave Woman herself rallied the warriors for a final charge. It was delivered with such fury that the Crow at last had to give way. This was the big battle in which the Crow Nation was driven away from the Missouri for good. It was a great victory, but many brave young men had died. Among the dead was Little Eagle, his face to the enemy. Red Horn's bow was broken, his eagle feathers taken from him. He was sent home. Little Eagle was placed on a high scaffold on the spot where the enemy camp had been. His horse was killed to serve him in the land of many lodges. "Go willingly," the horse was told. "Your master has need of you in the spirit world."

Brave Woman gashed her arms and legs with a sharp knife. She cut her hair short and tore her white buckskin dress. Thus she mourned for Little Eagle. They had not been man and wife. He had hardly ever dared to speak to her or look at her, but now she asked everybody to treat her as if she were the young warrior's widow. And the people did what she asked of them. Brave Woman never took a husband. She never ceased to mourn for Little Eagle. She told everyone, "I am his widow." She died of old age. She had done a very great thing. Her fame endures.

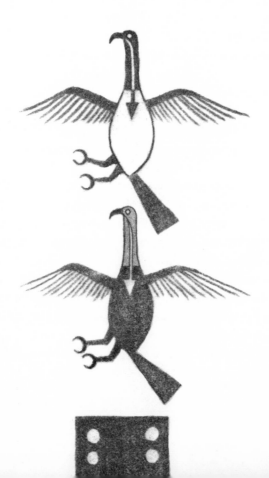

How the Crow Came To Be Black

Told by Good White Buffalo

In days long past, when the earth and the people on it were still young, all crows were white—as white as snow. In those ancient times, the people had neither horses nor firearms nor weapons of iron. Yet they depended upon the buffalo hunt to give them enough food to survive. Hunting the big buffalo on foot with stone-tipped weapons was hard, uncertain, and dangerous.

The crows made things even more difficult for the hunters because they were friends of the buffalo. Soaring high above the prairie, they could see everything that was going on. Whenever they spied hunters approaching a buffalo herd, they would fly to their friends, perching between their horns, warning them, "Caw, caw, caw, cousins, hunters are coming. They are creeping up through that gully over there. They are coming up behind that hill. Watch out! Caw, caw, caw!" Hearing this, the buffalo would stampede, and the people starved.

The people held a council to decide what to do. Now, among the crows was a huge one, twice as big as all the other crows.

This crow was their leader. One old, wise chief therefore got up and made this suggestion. "We must capture the big white crow," he said, "and teach him a lesson. It is either that or go hungry." He brought out a large buffalo skin with the head and horns still attached to it. He put it on the back of a young brave. "Nephew," he told him, "you will sneak among the buffalo. They will think you are one of them. You will capture the big crow."

Disguised as a buffalo, the young man crept among the herd as if he were grazing. The big, shaggy beasts paid him no attention. Then the hunters marched out from the village after him, their bows at the ready. As they approached the herd, the crows came flying, as usual, warning the buffalo, "Caw, caw, caw, cousins, the hunters are coming again to kill you. Watch out for their arrows. Caw, caw, caw!" And, as usual, all the buffalo galloped off and away—all, that is, except the young hunter in disguise under his shaggy skin, who pretended to go on grazing as before.

Then the big white crow came gliding down, perching on his shoulders, flapping his wings, saying, "Caw, caw, caw, brother, are you deaf? The hunters are close by, just over the hill. Save yourself!" But the young brave reached out from under the buffalo skin and grabbed the crow by its legs. With a rawhide string he tied the big crow up by the feet, fastening the other end to a stone. No matter how the crow struggled, it could not escape.

Again the people sat in council. "What shall we do with this bad, big crow, who has made us go hungry many times, again

and again?" "I will burn it up," answered one angry hunter, and before anybody could stop him, he tore the crow from the hands of the young man who had captured it. Getting hold of the stone, the angry hunter thrust the crow into the council fire, saying, "This will teach you."

Of course, the string that held the stone burned through almost at once, and the big crow managed to fly out of the fire. But it was badly singed, and some of its feathers were charred. It was still big, but it certainly was no longer white. "Caw, caw, caw," it cried, flying away as quickly as it could, "I'll never do it again, I'll stop warning the buffalo, I and all the Crow Nation. I promise. Caw, caw, caw."

Thus the crow escaped. But ever since that time, all crows are black.

Iktome and the Hawk

Told by Jake Herman

Iktome, the clever spider man, is a right smart creature. Sometimes too smart for his own good. Iktome was sitting on a log one fine morning, sunning himself, when he saw Cetan, the hawk, flying overhead. "Brother," Iktome called out, "give me a ride." The good-natured hawk let Iktome climb up on his back. Up in the air Iktome enjoyed the flight and the gorgeous view, but soon he was bored. Iktome is always bored unless he can play a joke on someone. He decided to have some fun at the hawk's expense.

Now, there are no cuss words in the Sioux language, no cuss words at all. But there is the sign language. With your hand and fingers you can make a sign to indicate that someone is a *Chlete* —a good-for-nothing so-and-so. Whenever they encountered an eagle, a buzzard, or a magpie on their flight, Iktome made this sign, which told these birds that the hawk was just a no-account,

60

no-good, stupid fellow. He thought that the hawk could not see him doing it. He was sitting on top of the hawk's head. Even hawks don't have eyes on the back of their skulls.

But the hawk could see his shadow on the ground, and saw very well how Iktome made fun of him. "I'll get even with this trickster," he thought. All of a sudden the hawk turned over, flying upside down, causing Iktome to lose his grip so that he fell through the air, landing inside a hollow tree. The trickster was still trying to find his way out of it when it began to rain. It rained very hard. The tree was very dry. It soaked up the water like a sponge and swelled up. Poor Iktome was being crushed to death.

Poor Iktome! In his pain and fear he began to pray, "Great Spirit, why did you make me so smart that I always try to fool everybody? In the end I am only fooling myself. Please save me." Thus Iktome humbled himself. His former pride and wickedness made him feel very small, so small that he was able to crawl out of that tree. A little humility, self-knowledge, and prayer can be a good thing sometimes.

The Vision Quest

Told by Lame Deer

Visions are important to the plains people. A man or woman trying to find the right way on their road of life, or trying to find the answer to a personal problem, might want to go on a vision quest to find knowledge and enlightenment. This often means staying on top of a lonely hill, or inside a vision pit, alone, without food or water, for as long as four days and nights. This is a hard thing to do, but if you hear the spirit voices telling you what to do, showing you a path out of your troubles, giving you a vision that will determine your life, then the quest is worth all the suffering you might endure.

The story is told of a young man who wanted to go on such a *hanbleceya*, or vision seeking, in order to cry out for a dream that would give him the power to be a great medicine man. This young fellow had a very high opinion of himself, thinking that he had been created to become great among his people and that the only thing lacking was a vision to bestow power upon him.

His relatives had faith in him, too. All through the winter

they were busy getting him ready, feeding him *wasna*—pemmican—corn, and plenty of good meat to make him strong for his ordeal. At every meal they set aside something for the spirits so that they would help this young man to get a great vision. He was daring and brave, eager to go up to the mountaintop. He was brought up by good, honest people who were wise in the ancient ways and who prayed for him. They thought he had the power even before he went up, but that was putting the cart before the horse—or rather, the *travois* before the horse, as this is an Indian legend.

When he started out, it was a beautiful day in late spring. The grass was up, the leaves were out—nature was at its best that morning. Two medicine men were with this young man to help him. They put up a sweatlodge for him, purifying him in the hot, white breath of the sacred steam. They sanctified the boy with incense of sweetgrass, rubbing his body with sage, fanning it with an eagle's wing. They went to the hilltop with him, preparing the vision pit, making an offering of tobacco bundles. The medicine men told the young man to cry, to humble himself; they said to ask for holiness, to cry for power, for a sign from the Great Spirit, for a gift that would make him into a medicine man. After they had done all they could, they left him there alone.

He spent the first night in the hole that the medicine men had dug for him, trembling, crying out loudly, fear keeping him awake—yet he was cocky, ready to wrestle with the spirits for the vision, the power he wanted. But no dreams came to him to ease his mind. Toward morning, before the sun came up, in swirling white mists of dawn he heard a voice speaking to him from no particular direction, as if it came from several different places, "See here, young man, there are other spots you could

64

have picked, there are other hills around here. Why don't you go there to cry for a dream? You were disturbing us all night, all us creatures, animals and birds—you even kept the trees awake. We couldn't sleep. Why should you cry here? You are a brash young man and not ready or worthy to receive a vision yet." But the young man just clenched his teeth, determined to stick it out, resolved to force that vision to come to him.

He spent another day in the pit, begging for enlightenment that would not come, and then another night of fear and cold and hunger. When dawn arrived once more, he heard the voices again, "Stop this! Go away!" And the same thing happened to him on the third morning. By this time he was faint with hunger, thirst, and anxiety. Even the air seemed to oppress him, to fight him. He was panting. His stomach felt shriveled up, shrunk tight against his backbone. But he was determined to endure one more night, the fourth and last. Surely the vision would come during it. Again he cried for it out of the dark and loneliness until he was hoarse—and still no dream came.

Just before daybreak he heard the same voices again, sounding angry, asking, "Why are you still here?" He knew then that he had suffered in vain, and that hurt him, because now he would have to go back to his people telling them that he had gained no knowledge and no power. The only thing he could tell them was that he got bawled out every morning and that made him sad and cross. So he talked back to those voices. "I cannot help

myself, this is my last day and I am crying my eyes out. I know you told me to go home, but who are you to tell me? I don't know you. I am going to stay here until my uncles come later to fetch me. Till then, I am staying whether you like it or not."

All at once there was a big rumble. Now, behind this hill there was a larger mountain, and the rumble came from there. It turned into a mighty frightening roar. The whole hill trembled. The wind started to blow. The young man looked up and saw a big boulder poised on the mountain's summit. He saw lightning hit it, saw it sway. Slowly the boulder moved, slowly at first and then faster and faster. It came tumbling down the mountainside, churning up the earth, snapping huge trees in two as if they were little twigs. And the boulder *was coming right down on him!*

The young man cried out in terror. He was paralyzed with fear, unable to move. The boulder dwarfed everything in view— it towered over the vision pit—but just as it was about to crush him, a mere arm's length away, it suddenly stopped. Then, as the young man stared open-mouthed, the hair on his head standing up, his eyes starting out of his head, the boulder *rolled up the mountain,* all the way to the top. The young man could hardly believe what he saw. He was still cowering motionless when he heard the roar and rumble again and saw that immense boulder coming down at him once more. This time he managed to jump out of his vision pit at the last moment as the boulder crushed and obliterated it, grinding into dust the peace pipe and gourd rattle which the young man had brought for his vision quest.

Again the boulder rolled up the mountain and again it came down. "I am leaving, I am leaving!" hollered the young man, who had finally regained his power of motion and was scrambling down the hill as well and as fast as he could. This time the

boulder actually leap-frogged over him, bouncing down the
slope, crushing and pulverizing everything in its way. The young
man ran and ran, unseeing, stumbling, falling, getting up again.
He did not even notice the boulder rolling up once more and
coming down finally for the fourth and last time. On this last
and most fearful descent, the boulder leaped through the air in
a giant bounce, bedding itself deeply in the earth so that only its
top was visible, right in front of the young man. The whole hill
and the ground all around shook itself like a wet dog coming
out of a stream, flinging the young man this way and that.

He stumbled into his village gaunt, bruised, and shaken. To
the medicine men he said, "I have received no vision and gained
no knowledge. I have made the spirits angry. It was all for
nothing."

"Well, you did find out one thing," said the older of the two
medicine men, an uncle. "You went after your vision like a
hunter after buffalo, or a warrior after scalps. You were fighting
the spirits. You thought they owed you a vision. Suffering alone
brings no vision, nor does courage or sheer will power. A vision
comes as a gift born from humility, from wisdom, and from
patience. If from your vision quest you have learned nothing but
this, then you have already learned much. Think about it."

Mice Powwow in an Elk Skull

Told by Strange Owl

Veeho, the no-good trickster, was married. He was not a good husband. He used to beat his wife often and without reason. "One day," she thought, "I am going to get even with him."

One fine morning, Veeho was going for a walk when he heard a thin, piping, squeaking noise. It was very strange, very high-pitched; but it was also a nice sound, a melody from another world. Veeho followed the sound and found that it came from the bleached skull of a big elk. Veeho peeked inside the skull through one of the empty eye sockets. What he saw astounded him.

The skull was the home of a tribe of mice, the tiniest mice he had ever seen. And they were having a big powwow! They had a cooking fire going, with a stewpot dangling over it. And a big toad was there, lying on its back, letting its belly be used as a drum by four mice who beat upon it with tiny sticks. They were singing songs of the Mouse Nation with their squeaky little voices, and all the other mice danced: the Stomp Dance, the Grass Dance, the Omaha Dance, the Squaw Dance, and the Scalp Dance—every kind of dance.

Then, after the other mice had stopped singing, one mouse warrior came to the middle of the dance circle and began to sing. He sang, "I am a mighty warrior. Behold me. Cats I fear not. Owls I fear not. A hundred coups I counted upon cats. A thousand coups I counted upon owls. Who will stand against me?" All the mice jumped up and let out a mighty roar—mighty for mice, that is, a squeaking roar, rather—shouting, "Indeed, this is a great warrior, hau, hau!" Then the mouse warrior performed a fancy dance with many tiny, intricate steps, wonderful to behold, while the drummers beat the toad's belly in a frenzy.

Veeho was all excited. He could not remain still any longer. He squeezed the tip of his nose inside the skull, saying, "Cousins, let me come in, let me join you in your wonderful powwow."

The mice were astonished to see the tip of his big nose. They were surprised to hear his big voice. "No, no, no," they cried. "You cannot come in. You are too large, too tall, too wide, too fat, too everything to come in here."

Now Veeho always hangs around medicine men, trying to get some of their power, and one of these holy ones had given him a little power to make himself small and get into tight places. He used this power now, but it was really not much, just enough to get his head inside the skull. As soon as the mice saw his face threatening to fill up their bony home, they all fled, escaping through cracks in the skull, even the mouse warrior who had counted coup on cats and owls. How they squeaked!

Veeho, who is very clever but not very wise, had asked the medicine man to give him a little power to get into small places, but he had forgotten to ask for power to get out. He found that he was stuck. He could not get the elk skull off his head. He staggered home to his wife shouting, "Help me get this thing off!"

His wife came running. She thought, "Now I shall get even

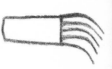

69

with this no-good husband of mine." She tugged and tugged, almost tearing his ears off.

"Ow, ow, stop," he howled. "You are hurting me."

"I guess I will have to knock it off," she said. "I will have to break this elk's skull to get you free. It is the only way."

"Yes, yes," he cried, "only hurry."

The wife got a big stick and started beating on the skull. Often she missed—on purpose—so that her blows landed on his back and shoulders. She gave Veeho a good thrashing.

"Ow, ow, ow," he wailed. "Be more careful."

"You are moving about so much, you make me miss my aim," she answered hitting him again. At last she broke the skull in two with her heavy stick. "Don't put your head in any more skulls!"

"I won't," said Veeho.

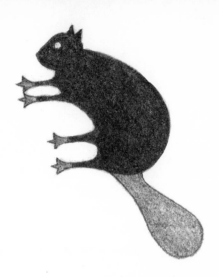

The Fastest Animal,
the Fastest Man, the Fastest Story

Told by Lame Deer

This, you might say, is a modern legend. A man, and what his name was is forgotten now, wanted to hunt a certain kind of gopher. Now, this kind is the fastest animal on earth. The moment you raise your bow or gun, this animal disappears into its gopher hole. Even when hit, even when it is already dead, it still makes a last leap to be swallowed up in its hole. So the man was told by his uncle, "If you want that gopher, shoot real quick and then run, run like hell to catch him before he puts on his vanishing act." The man did as he was told. He saw the gopher. Quick as lightning, he raised his gun and fired. Just as quickly he ran. As he stretched out his hand to catch the gopher, he received a terrific blow in the seat of his pants. He had outrun his own bullet, and it had hit him. From then on, he was known as Swift Runner. He deserved his new name, don't you think?

How the Sioux Nation Came into Being

Told by Lame Deer

This is a story one of my Santee relatives told me. You know, there are many tribes of the Sioux. The seven western tribes are called the Lakota. They speak Lakota. They can pronounce an *L*, but cannot pronounce a *D*. The eastern Sioux tribes are called Dakota. They speak Dakota. They can pronounce a *D*, but cannot pronounce an *L*. So we have a joke about them. Question: "What is a flat tire in Dakota?" Answer: "a bDow-out." Well, the Santees are Dakotas. They speak our language perfectly, except that they aDways use a *D* when taDking their Danguage, instead of an *L*. But they are our good cousins, and we understand each other perfectly. Well, my Santee cousins have a story of how the Sioux Nation was born. Here it is.

Untold generations ago, when the world was freshly made, a great flood came and covered all the earth—all of it, that is, except the hills near where our sacred pipestone quarries are. The Indian people fled to the top of these hills, but the flood continued to rise and rise. Finally, the waves swept over the hills, killing all the people there. Their flesh and blood were turned into pipestone and that is why the pipe is so sacred to us—it is made of the red rock, the flesh of our ancestors.

As the waters engulfed the hills, a big eagle swooped down from the sky and let a beautiful young girl grab hold of its legs. It carried her to safety to the top of a tall tree that rose from the highest cliff above the prairies, the only dry spot between the Rocky Mountains and the Great Eastern Ocean.

In time the beautiful young girl became the great eagle's wife. After a while the young woman gave birth to twins, a boy and a girl. The great eagle was their father. They were born right on top of that high cliff, after the great flood subsided. The twins grew up and began a new tribe of people—the Sioux Nation. It was to become a famous tribe of brave and strong people whose deeds became part of the history of this country.

The sacred peace pipe reminds us of the Sioux Nation's birth. So does the pipestone quarry, which still is open to all Indians; they get the red rock for their pipe bowls there. So does the eagle feather, proudly worn by young Sioux men; yesterday and today, the eagle feather says, "I am Sioux, I am Indian and proud of it, I will do good things for my people."

The Coming of Wasicun

Told by Leonard Crow Dog

Many generations ago, Iktome, the spider man, trickster and bringer of bad news, went from village to village and from tribe to tribe. Because he is a messenger, Iktome can speak any language, so that all tribes can understand what he says.

He came running into the first camp shouting, "There is a new generation coming, a new nation, a new kind of man who is going to run everything. He is like me, Ikto, a trickster, a prankster, a liar. He has two long legs with which he will run over you."

Iktome asked for all the chiefs to gather in council. This was done, and the head chief asked, "Ikto, what news do you bring from the east?"

Iktome answered, "There is a new man coming, he is like me, but he has long, long legs and many new things, most of them

74

bad. And he is clever like me. I want to tell all the tribes about him." Then the spider man sang, "I am Iktome and I roll with the air."

Iktome then left the council. Three young boys followed him out of curiosity to see where he was going. They watched him climb to the top of a hill where he made his body shrink into a ball, changing himself from a man into a spider. The boys saw a silvery spider web against the blueness of the sky, with a single strand from it that led down to the hill. The boys watched Iktome climb into the web and disappear in the sky.

The next tribe Iktome visited were the *Lakota*—the Sioux Nation. Two old women gathering firewood saw him standing on a butte near their village. They went home and told the chief, "We saw this strange man standing over there, looking at us."

The chief called for two of his four *wakincuzas*—the pipe-owners, the ones who decide—and said to them, "Bring this strange man to me. Maybe he brought a message."

They brought Ikto into the camp. He appeared to them in the shape of a human being. He stretched out his hand toward the sun, saying, "I am Iktome. I roll with the air. I have to bring my message to seventy-five villages. This is what I have come to tell you. A sound is coming from the edge of the sea. It is coming from *pankeska*, the seashell. It is the voice of *pankeska hoksi unpapi*, the Shell Nation. One cannot tell from where this voice is coming, the north or the south, but it is telling us that a

new man is approaching, the *Hu-Hanska-Ska,* the white spider man, the daddy-longlegs-man. He is coming across the Great Water, coming to steal all the four directions of the world."

"How will we know him?" asked the chief and the wakincuzas.

"Each of his long legs will be a leg of knowledge, of *wounspe.* This new man is not wise, but he is very clever. He has knowledge in his legs. Wherever these legs step, they will make a track of lies; and wherever he looks, his looks will be all lies. At this time, you must try to know and understand this new kind of man, pass this understanding on from generation to generation. This message is carried by the wind."

Iktome made his body into a small ball with eight legs, and from the sky there appeared the fine strand of a spider web, glistening with dewdrops. On it, Iktome climbed up into the clouds and disappeared.

Iktome next went to the village of the *Mapiya-To,* the blue-cloud people, who are also known as the Arapaho. Again the chiefs and the people came to ask what news he was bringing, and he spoke to them in their own language. "I have brought you a bundle to open up, and my news is in it. The Iktome-Hu-Hanska-Ska is coming, the white longlegs. I flew through the air to bring you this message. This new kind of man comes walking."

The Arapaho chief asked, "How is it that you fly and he walks?"

"*Wokahta,*" said Iktome, "is traveling slowly, going gradually from the east toward the south and west, eating up whole nations, devouring the whole earth."

The chief asked, "When is he going to be here?"

"You will know by the star. When you see a double star, one star reflecting another, then the Hu-Hanska-Ska is near."

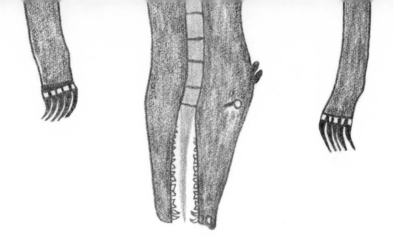

Iktome went away. He passed two women who were out in the prairie looking for *timpsila*, wild turnips. They were using deer horns for digging. They saw Iktome on the flat, walking, pointing his arm skyward. All of a sudden he drew himself up into a ball. At the same time, the thread of a spider web from up high hit the earth, and Iktome climbed onto it and vanished in the air.

Near the village of the *Kangi Wicasa*—the Crow People—two old men were digging for Indian medicine. They saw a stranger standing behind a tree. They saw him circling the camp. They said to each other, "He is not from our tribe. Let us ask him what he wants."

Ikto spoke to them in the Crow tongue. "The white longlegs is coming. Look around you at the things you see, the grass, the trees, the animals, the Iktome Hu-Hanska-Ska will take them all. He will steal the air. He will give you a new, different life, he will give you many new things. But hold on to your old ways; mind what *Tunkashila*, the grandfather spirit, taught you."

The two old men said, "We better bring you to our chief." And they did so.

The Crow chief asked Iktome, "What message have you for us?'"

77

"The white longlegs is coming. He will eat up the grass, and the trees, and the buffalo. He will bring you a new faith. I am telling you this, I, Ikto, who rolls with the air."

The Crow chief asked, "Why is he coming? We do not want him here. We do not want his new things. We have everything here to make us happy."

"He will come," said Iktome, "whether you want him or not. He is coming from the east."

"How is it that your name is Ikto?"

"Because I am Iktome, the spider man. Remember this tree of the white ash. It is sacred. *Iya, Tunka.* Remember the rock. The rocks are forever."

One Crow woman gave Iktome a handful of *wasna*, jerky meat mixed with kidney fat and berries, to take with him on his travels. Iktome thanked her, saying, "You must watch this new man. Whatever he does and says and asks, say 'Hiya' to him: say 'No'; say 'Hiya' to everything. Now I take my message to the west, to *Wiyopeyata*."

Iktome stood in the center of the tipi circle. All the Crow chiefs were standing around him wearing their war bonnets. Suddenly, a great surge of power was felt by all. Iktome shrank into a ball, and the thread of a spider web that was floating in the sky hit the prairie causing a trembling and thundering deep inside the earth. While all marveled, Iktome climbed up the thread into the web and was gone.

A man was wandering through a valley. He was seen by a warrior getting his horses together. This warrior was a *susuni* of the snake people, who are also known as Shoshone. He asked the

man why he had come. The stranger said, "I am Ikto. I roll with the air. I come from *Wiyohiyanpata*—the east—a generation coming with news."

The warrior said, "Stay here. I will bring our chief."

The Shoshone chief came, followed by his people. Ikto told him, "A new kind of man is coming, a white longlegs with many lies and many new things. If you want them, that is up to you."

The chief put two sticks on the ground facing north and south. It was a symbol for saying no. "We don't want him," answered the chief. "Our generation is good, our nation is good, our land is good. No, we do not want this new kind of man."

Ikto told him, "He will come anyhow. I am going *Waziyata*—toward the north—to bring my message to the people there."

Ikto climbed a hill, and the Shoshone people saw lightning strike the summit and heard the sound of many buffalo in the earth beneath their feet.

Iktome reappeared in the North, walking toward the village of the *Pahani*, or Pawnees. Pointing his finger to their camp, he shouted, "A new generation, a new kind of man is coming to this world."

One old Pahani woman asked, "Is it a newborn child?"

"No," said Ikto, "it is no child, but a man without grand-mothers or grandfathers, a man bringing new sicknesses and worries."

79

"We do not want him, what shall we do?" the Pawnees asked.

"You, yourselves, must know what to do. I am going back to my people."

The Pawnees said, "Don't go yet."

Iktome went toward the north, holding a pine bough in his hand, pointing it in the four directions, up to the Grandfather Sky and the Grandmother Earth. "Remember, this will be the plant of worship in the center of the earth and with it you will see and know."

Everybody said yes—*ohan*—in their own language.

Iktome went back to the Sioux people. He flew through the air to their camp. The wind carried him. He told the people, "I am going back into the sea. That new man is coming. He is almost here. I will reveal to you his name."

"How will he come?" asked the Sioux chief.

"He is coming in a *wate*, a boat. You are the *Ikce Wicasa*—the plain, wild people—but he will misname you and call you by all kinds of false names. He will try to tame you, to remake you after himself. This man will lie. Always he will lie, for he cannot tell the truth."

"When is he going to come?"

"When the white flower blooms. Watch the buffalo. Sooner or later the white longlegs will be here and will take all the buffalo. He will bring four things: *wicocuye*, sickness; *wawoya*, hate; *wawiwagele-sni*, prejudice; and *waunshilap-sni*, pitilessness. He will try to give you a new Great Spirit—*Naha Wico Wakan*—

making you exchange your own *Wakan Tanka* for a new god and thereby lose the world. But always remember Tunka, the rock. He has no mouth, no eyes, no ears, but he has the power. Hold on to it.

"And always remember Tunkashila, the Grandfather, the Great Spirit. This new man is coming, coming to live among you. He will lie, and his lie never ends. He is going to make a dark, black hoop around the world."

"Is there no hope?" the people asked.

"Maybe and maybe not. I do not know. First it will happen as I told you, and with his long legs he will run over you. Maybe a time will come when you can break this dark hoop. Maybe you can change this man and make him like you, giving him earth-wisdom, making him listen to what the grass and the trees could tell him. But maybe he will just eat up everything. You shall know him by his name—*Wasi-Manu*, Steal-All—or better by the name *Wasicun*, Fat-Taker, because he will take the fat of the land—at least for a time."

The Very Angry Ghost

Told by Spotted Elk

Young men never know how to behave themselves. They should learn good manners from their elders, but they seldom do.

One day, long ago, an old warrior who had counted many coups in his days took three young braves with him on a raid to steal horses from the Pawnees, ancient enemies of the Sioux.

"Stealing horses"—this is what the white men call it. But it was really a sport practiced by all the Plains tribes. To creep into an enemy village noiselessly, unseen, and to make off with their herd right under the noses of the horse guards—to outwit, out-think, and outride them—took great skill and brought fame and honor to a warrior.

On this raid, though, the four Sioux had no luck. They were discovered by the enemy before they could even get near the horse herd. They had to be happy to get out of this scrape alive by running away and hiding themselves in a ravine. They had left on foot, and on foot they went home. Their moccasins had holes in them from their many days of hard walking. They were hungry, tired, and empty-handed.

Halfway home, they passed a hill on top of which they spied a lonely tipi, all by itself, and without any signs of life. They wondered what it was doing there on the wild prairie, and went up to investigate. They found that it was a burial tipi—a splendid one made of sixteen large buffalo hides and painted all over with pictures of war and hunting.

Inside they found the body of a man, his face painted in the sacred scarlet color, lying in state in a resplendent war shirt and beautifully beaded leggings. His fine weapons, his quilled moccasins, and all his other possessions were spread about him to take along to the spirit world.

The young men looked admiringly at all these fine things. "What a stroke of luck," they said. "We will take all this to bring home, turning failure into success."

"A fine success," chided the old warrior. "To steal horses from an enemy brings honor, but to rob the dead is shameful. How wrong I was to pick youths of low mind like you to accompany me. Don't you know that only great chiefs and famous warriors are buried thus?"

They left and went down the hill again, making their camp near a stream. But the young men were still thinking of all the splendid things left in the lone tipi. "I think it was stupid to leave it all there," said one of them. "We should have taken everything," said the second. "Let us go right now and do it," said the third.

"I really showed bad judgment in picking you to go with me on a raid," the old man told them. "I will never be able to make good warriors out of you!"

But the young men would not listen. "Old one, show some sense," they answered him. "Those fine things are of no use to one who is dead, but they are of much use to us who are alive."

"Well, I guess you better go without me then," said the old warrior. So they left him to go up that hill again. Quickly the old man ran to the stream and smeared himself all over with cold mud. He took a fur pouch he wore, made two holes in it, and put it over his head as a mask. He looked like a ghost from another world. He ran fast, circling the hill, coming up on the far side, and sat down in the entrance of the lone tipi before the three young braves arrived.

When they got there, they heard an eerie hollow voice, resounding from the tipi. "Who has come here to rob a great chief? I will take them to the spirit world with me." Out from under the entrance flap rose the specter of a frightful ghost, the pale moonlight making it look still more terrible to the young men, who were so petrified with fright that their hair stood on end. They stood stock-still and open-mouthed for a few seconds. Then, all together, they dropped their bows, turned around, and took to their heels, running down the hill as fast as their feet would carry them.

It was not very fast. They were so scared, they didn't know where to put their feet. They stumbled, they stepped on cactus and prickly pear, they got stuck in the underbrush. The ghost got nearer and nearer, gaining on them fast. At last the hindmost felt a cold, clammy hand touching his bare shoulder and a hollow voice whispering in his ear, "Friend, I have come for

you!" The young man was so frightened he fell down in a dead faint.

Then it was the next young man's turn to feel the icy hand, and to hear the ghostlike voice. He, too, fainted. And so did the third and last one.

The old man got back to the campsite well ahead of them. He took off his mask and washed the mud from his body in the cold stream. He was warming himself by the fire as the bedraggled young men came in one by one.

"Where are all those fine things you wanted to take from that dead chief?" asked the old warrior.

"We did not find the tipi," said the young men. "And we did not feel like taking those things after all."

The old warrior said nothing.

Back home in their village, the three young men were sitting in the camp circle telling the people about their raid. Suddenly the old warrior came and sat down among the others. He put on his fur mask and laid a muddy hand on a pretty girl's shoulder. "Does that frighten you, *wincincala?*" he asked the girl.

"You are a funny old man," said the girl, giggling.

"There are some here who were very frightened," said the old warrior, "so frightened that they fainted." And he told the story of how he had fooled them.

Everybody had a good laugh at the young men's expense. They were shamed, but this was good for them. It taught them a lesson, how to act and how to behave, so that they turned out to be good men and brave warriors.

Doing a Trick with Eyeballs

Told by Rachel Strange Owl

Veeho, the naughty trickster, is like some tourists who come into an Indian village not knowing how to behave or what to do, trying to impress everybody. Veeho is like that.

One day Veeho met a medicine man with great powers. This man thought to amuse Veeho—and himself—with a little trick. "Eyeballs," he shouted, "I command you to fly out of my head and hang on that branch over there, on that tree." At once his eyeballs shot out of his head and in a flash were hanging from a branch. Veeho watched open-mouthed. "Good, good, eyeballs," cried the medicine man. "Now come back where you belong!" And, quick as lightning, the eyeballs were back where they belonged.

"Uncle," said Veeho, "please give me a little of your power so that I can do this wonderful trick." To himself, Veeho thought, "If he will give me this power, then I will play medicine man, and impress people no end, especially the pretty girls, and find many ways to turn this to my advantage." But he did not say this aloud.

"Why not?" said the medicine man. "Why not give you a little power to please you? But let me warn you, Veeho. Do not use this trick more than four times a day, or your eyeballs won't come back."

"I won't," said Veeho.

Veeho could hardly wait to get away by himself and try out this stunning trick. As soon as he was alone, he ordered, "Eyeballs, hop on that ledge over there. Jump to it!" And the eyeballs did.

Veeho couldn't see a thing. "Quickly, eyeballs, back into your sockets!" Again the eyeballs obeyed. "Boy, oh boy," Veeho thought to himself, "what a big man I am. Powerful, really powerful." Soon he saw another tree. "Eyeballs, up into this tree. Quick!" For a second time the eyeballs did as they were told. "Back into the skull!" Veeho shouted, snapping his fingers. And once more the eyeballs performed as they were told. Veeho was enjoying himself hugely. He was getting used to this marvelous trick. He couldn't stop. Twice more he performed it. "Well, that's it for today," he told himself.

Later in the day he came to a big village. How he wanted to impress the people with his powers. "Would you believe it, cousins," he told them, "I can make my eyeballs jump out of my head, fly over to that tree, hang themselves from a branch, and come back when I tell them." The people, of course, did not believe this and made fun of him. Veeho grew angry. "It is true, it is true," he cried. "You stupid people. I can do it."

"Show us," said the people.

"How often have I done this trick?" Veeho tried to remember. "Four times? No, no. The first time was only for practice. It doesn't count. I can still show these yokels something." And he commanded, "Eyeballs, hang yourself up in a branch of that

87

tree over there!" The eyeballs did, and a great cry of wonder and astonishment went up. "There, you stupid folks, didn't I tell you?" said Veeho, strutting around, puffing out his cheeks, clicking his heels. After a while he said, "All right, eyeballs, come back." But the eyeballs stayed up in the tree. "Come back, come back, you no-good eyeballs!" Veeho cried again and again. But the eyeballs stayed put no matter how the trickster carried on. Finally a big, fat crow came and gobbled them up. "Mm, good," said the crow. "Very tasty." The people laughed at the trickster, shook their heads, and went away.

Veeho was blind now. He didn't know what to do. He groped his way through a forest. He sat down by a rock and cried. He heard a squeaking noise. It was a mouse calling to other mice. "Mouse, little mouse," cried Veeho, "I am blind. Please lend me one of your eyes so that I can see again."

"My eyes are tiny," answered the mouse, "much too tiny. What good would one of them be to you? It wouldn't fit." But Veeho begged so pitifully that the mouse finally gave him one of her eyes, saying, "I guess I can get along with the other one."

So Veeho had one eye, but it was so very small—as small, well, as small as a mouse's eye. And the image he saw was just as small, just a little speck of light. Still, it was better than nothing.

Veeho staggered on and met a buffalo. "Buffalo, buffalo," he implored, "I have to get along with just a tiny mouse eye. How can a big man like me make do with that? Have pity on me, uncle, and lend me one of your beautiful big eyes."

"What good would one of my eyes do you?" asked the buffalo. "It is much too big for your eye hole." But Veeho begged and wept and wheedled until the buffalo at last said, "Well, all right, I'll let you have one. I can't stand listening to you carrying on like that. I guess I can get by with one eye."

And so Veeho had his second eye. The buffalo bull's eye was much too big. It protruded out of its socket like a shinny ball boys like to play with. It was really huge. With it Veeho saw everything twice as big as with his own eyes. But what could he do? It was better than no eye. It gave him a headache, though.

Veeho came back to his wife and lodge. His wife looked at him. "I believe your eyes are a little mismatched," she told him. And he described to her all that had happened to him. "You know," she said, "I think you should stop all this fooling around and playing tricks and trying to impress people."

"I guess so," said Veeho.

The Eagle and the Bat

Told by Lame Deer

Once all the birds came together in a big powwow. They played games to see who could fly the fastest and had other contests. At the end they said, "Now let's see which of us can fly higher than all the others." The kite, the hawk, the falcon, the wild goose, the crane—they all flew so high that they almost disappeared from sight. But then *Wanblee*, the eagle, spread his mighty wings and soared up into the air, higher than any other bird, almost all the way up to the sun.

When Wanblee finally came down again, all the birds set up a trilling, high-pitched honoring cry, saying, "The eagle beat us all. He can fly the highest!"

But just then a little bat popped up from out of the plumes on the top of Wanblee's head, flapping its puny leather wings and yelling, "No, no, I flew higher than Wanblee, hiding myself on top of his head. Being on top of Wanblee, naturally I was higher up than he or anybody else."

For this presumption and trickery, the birds transformed the bat into a mouse, taking away his wings. "From now on," said the eagle, "you'll stay in a hole beneath the earth, and the owl will watch so that you won't dare come out of your hole until you learn how to behave yourself."

Iktome and the Ducks

Told by Lame Deer

One day Iktome, the wicked spider man, was taking a walk to see what he could see. Tiptoeing through the woods, he saw water sparkling through the leaves. "I am coming to a lake," Iktome said to himself. "There might be some fat ducks there. I shall creep up to this lake very carefully so that I cannot be seen. Maybe I shall catch something."

Iktome crept up to the water's edge on all fours, hiding himself behind some bushes. Sure enough, the lake was full of nice, plump ducks. At the sight of them Iktome's mouth began to water. But how was he to catch the birds? He had neither a net nor his bow and arrows. But he had a stick. He suddenly popped up from behind the bushes, capering and dancing.

"Ho, cousins, come here and learn to dance. I have eight legs and I am the best dancer in the world."

All the ducks swam to the shore and lined up in a row, spellbound by Iktome's fancy dancing. After a while Iktome stopped. "Cousins, come closer still," he cried. "I am the gentle, generous spider man, the friend of all fowl, and I shall teach you the duck song. Now, when I start singing, you must all close your eyes in order to concentrate better. Do not peek while I sing, or you will be turned into ugly mudhens with red eyes. You don't want this

to happen, do you. You have, no doubt, noticed my stick. It is a drumstick which I will use to beat out the rhythm. Are you ready? Then close your eyes."

Itkome started to sing, and the foolish ducks crowded around him, doing as he had told them, flapping their wings delightedly and swaying to and fro. And with his stick Iktome began to club them dead, one after another.

Among the ducks was one young, smart one. "I better check on what is going on," this duck said to himself. "I don't quite trust that fellow with his eight legs. I'll risk one eye. One red eye isn't so bad." He opened his left eye and in a flash saw what Iktome was up to. "Take off, take off," he cried to the other ducks, "or we all wind up in the cooking pot!" The ducks opened their eyes and flew away, quacking loudly.

Still, Iktome had a fine breakfast of roast duck. The spider man's power turned the smart young duck into a mudhen.

This is why, to this day, mudhens swim alone, away from other ducks, always on the lookout, diving beneath the water as soon as they see or hear anyone approaching, thinking it might be the wicked spider man with a new bag of tricks. Better a live, ugly mudhen, than a pretty, dead duck.

The Owl and the Young Warrior

Told by Henry Crow Dog

The owl is a messenger. The owl is wise. If an owl warns you, heed her. Hinhan Win, the owl woman, sits in the middle of the big road called *Ta-canku*, which the white people call the Milky Way. The souls of the dead must walk along the Milky Way to reach the happy hunting grounds. Even today, most Indians have a little tattoo mark on their hands and wrists, even if these are no more than a few blue dots. When their souls, or spirits, want to pass, the owl woman examines them to see if those marks are there. If not, she will throw the soul down from the Milky Way. Those tattooes are an Indian's passport to the spirit world. Without them, they will not get past her.

Well, a young warrior was sent to scout an enemy village. He was on his third day out. He had put up a small tipi for himself, just about shoulder high. In it he had a bowl of water, a very small fire, and his weapons. He had eaten a sage hen he had shot with his arrows and was waiting for the moon to rise to go on his way. In the meantime, he was preparing a few new arrows because he was in enemy country and might have a sudden need for them.

While he was straightening his arrow shafts, he heard the sudden cry of Hinhan the owl, "Whoo, whoo, whoo." It came so abruptly that it startled him, and he dropped an arrowhead into the bowl of water before him. He bent over to retrieve it. As he did so, he saw, reflected in the water, the face of an enemy scout watching through the smokehole above him. He went on as before, as if he had not seen his enemy. But suddenly, in a flash, he twisted around and shot an arrow up through the watching face.

The young scout had killed his first enemy and counted his first coup. He had earned his first eagle feather. And, oh yes, his scouting was entirely successful, and he came back to his people with all the information they needed. The owl had saved his life. When Hinhan Win calls, for better or for worse, it is wise to pay attention.

The Ghostly Lover

Told by Lame Deer

We Sioux have all kinds of songs we like to sing. Some of them are ghost songs. I am thinking of one in particular, which is still known to a few old-timers like myself. Here is the story that goes with this song.

Long ago, there lived a young, good-looking man whom no woman could resist. He was an elk charmer, a man who had elk medicine which has the love power. When this young man played the *Siyotanka*—the flute—at night, its sound was like magic. A girl hearing it would get up and go to him. She would forsake her father and mother, her own lover or husband. Maybe her mind told her to stay, but her heart was already beating faster and her feet running. She had no control over them once she heard the flute. This young man with the elk charm did not really care for women. He had a stone heart. He just wanted to conquer women the way a warrior conquers an enemy. After the women came to him once, he had no more use for them. He did not act as a young man should—and as you can imagine, he was not very well liked.

95

One day the young man went out to hunt buffalo, but he never returned to the village. His parents waited for him, day after day, but he never came back. At last they asked a medicine man to find him. We have a special kind of medicine man whose gift is finding lost objects, even persons who have disappeared. It was to such a one that the parents went, and he used his finding stones on their behalf.

After the medicine man had held his ceremony, he told the parents, "I have sad news for you. Your son is dead. He did not die of sickness or an accident. He was killed. He is lying out there, on the prairie." The medicine man described to them the spot where they would find the body, and they went there. It was as the medicine man had said. The young man was lying there, dead, stabbed through the heart. They put his body up on the funeral scaffold dressed in his finest war shirt which he had liked so much because he had been vain, and put on him dead man's moccasins which have their soles decorated with beaded designs. Then the tribe left this part of the country, for it was a very bad thing, this killing of one tribal member by another, the very worst thing, even though everybody knew that the young man had brought it upon himself.

One evening, many a day's ride away, when the people were busy feasting and talking, having already forgotten this sad happening, all the dogs in the village started to howl mournfully, and all the coyotes out in the hills took up their melancholy cry. Nobody could find a reason for this fearful din, and when it stopped, one could hear instead the hooting of many owls, a hooting of death and ghostly things. The people got very uneasy about this. The laughter stopped. The fires were put out, and all went into their tipis, closing the entrance flaps behind them, trying to sleep, but trying in vain.

The people were listening. They knew a spirit was coming, and finally they heard the unearthly sounds of a ghost flute and a voice only too familiar to them. It was the voice of the dead young man with the elk medicine. They heard it singing:

Weeping I roam.
I thought I was the only one.
I thought I was the only one who had known many loves,
Many girls.
Now I am having a hard time.
I am roaming,
And I have to keep roaming,
As long as the world stands.

After that night, the people heard this song many times. A lone girl coming home late from a dance, a young woman up before sunrise to get water from a stream, would hear this song mixed with the sound of the flute and see the shape of a man hovering above the ground, wrapped in a gray blanket. Even as a ghost this young man would not leave the girls alone.

Well, it all happened a long time ago, but even now, the old-timers at Rosebud, Pine Ridge, and Cheyenne River still sing this song.

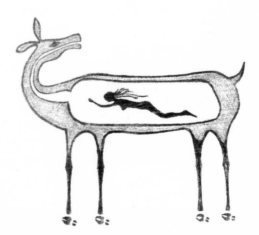

97

The Rabbit Boy

Told by Jenny Leading Cloud

This is the story of Rabbit Boy—*we-ota-wichasha*—which, if you translate it, means blood-much-man. In some tribes it is known as the story of the Blood-Clot Boy. As you know, we Indians think of this earth and the whole universe as a never-ending circle in which all living things are related to one another. In this circle man is just another animal. The buffalo and the coyote are our brothers; the birds, our cousins. Even the tiniest ant, even a louse, even the smallest flower you could find—they are all relatives. We end all our prayers with the words *mitakuye oyasin*—all my relations—and that includes everything that crawls, runs, creeps, hops, flies, and grows on this turtle continent. White people see man as nature's master and conqueror; but Indians, who are really close to nature, know better.

In the old, old days, before Columbus "discovered" us, as they say, we were still much closer to the animals than we are now. Many people could understand the animal languages; they could talk to a bird, gossip with a butterfly. Animals could change themselves into people, and people into animals. It was a time when the earth was not quite finished yet, when many kinds of mountains and streams, animals and plants came into being according to nature's plan.

In these far-gone days, hidden from us as in a mist, there lived a rabbit, a very nice, lively, playful good-hearted rabbit. One day this rabbit was walking, enjoying himself, when he came across a clot of blood. How it got there nobody knows. It looked like a blister, a little bladder full of red liquid. Well, the playful rabbit began toying with that clot of blood, kicking it around as if it were a tiny ball.

Now, we Indians believe in *Takuskanskan*, the mysterious power of motion. Its spirit is in anything that moves. It animates things and makes them come alive. Well, the rabbit got into this strange moving power without even knowing it, and the motion of being kicked around, or rather the spirit of the motion —and I hope you can grasp what I mean by that—began to work on that little blob of blood so that it took shape, forming a little gut. The rabbit kicked it some more, and the blob began to grow tiny hands and arms. The rabbit nudged it a bit more, and suddenly it had eyes and a beating heart. In this way the rabbit, with the help of the mysterious moving power, formed a human being, a little boy. The rabbit called him we-ota-wichasha, but he is better known as Rabbit Boy.

The rabbit took him to his wife, and both of them loved this strange little boy as if he were their only son. They dressed him up in a beautiful buckskin shirt, which they painted with the sacred red color and decorated with designs made of porcupine quills. The boy grew up happily among the rabbits. When he had grown up into almost a young man, the old rabbit took him aside and said, "Son, I must tell you that you are not what you think

99

you are—a rabbit like me. You are a human. We love you and we hate to let you go, but you must go and find your own kind of people."

The Rabbit Boy started walking until he came to a village of human beings. In it he saw boys who looked like himself. He went into the village. The people could not help staring at this strange boy in his beautiful buckskin clothes. "Where are you from?" they asked him. "I am from another village," said the Rabbit Boy, but this was not true. There was no other village in the whole world. As I told you, the earth was still in its beginning.

In the village lived a beautiful girl who fell in love with the Rabbit Boy, not only for his fine clothes, but also for his good looks and his kind heart. Her people, too, wanted him to marry into the village, wanted a man with his great mystery power to live among them. And the Rabbit Boy had a vision. In it he was wrestling with the sun, racing the sun, playing hand games with the sun—and always winning.

But, Iktome, the wicked spider man, the mean trickster, prankster, and witch doctor, wanted that beautiful girl for himself. He began to say bad things about Rabbit Boy. "Look at him," Iktome said, "showing off his buckskin outfit to us who are too poor to have such fine things." And to the men he also said, "How come you want to let him marry a girl from among you?" He also told them, "I have a magic hoop to throw over that Rabbit Boy. It will make him helpless in case you want to fight him."

Several boys said, "Iktome is right." They were jealous of Rabbit Boy on account of his strange power, his wisdom and generosity. They began to fight Rabbit Boy. The spider man threw his magic hoop over him, rendering him helpless. But

Rabbit Boy was not really helpless, he just pretended to be, to amuse himself.

The village boys and young men overcame Rabbit Boy and tied him to a tree with rawhide thongs. All the time the evil spider man was encouraging them, "Let's take our butchering knives and cut him up!"

"Friends, *kola-pila*," said the Rabbit Boy, "if you are going to kill me, let me sing my death song first." And the Rabbit Boy sang:

> *Friends, friends,*
> *I have fought the sun.*
> *He tried to burn me up,*
> *But he could not do it.*
> *Even battling the sun,*
> *I held my own.*

After he had sung his death song, the villagers killed Rabbit Boy and cut him up into chunks of meat which they put in a soup pot. But Rabbit Boy was not hurt easily. A storm arose, and a great cloud hid the face of the sun, turning everything into black night.

When the cloud was gone, the chunks of meat had disappeared without a trace, but those who had watched closely had seen the chunks forming up again into a body, had seen him going up to heaven on a beam of sunlight. A wise old medicine  man said, "This Rabbit Boy really has very powerful medicine. He has gone up to see the sun. Soon he will come back stronger than before, because up there he will be given the power of the sun. Let us marry him to that girl of ours."

But, the jealous spider, Iktome, said, "Why bother about him, look at me. I am much more powerful than that Rabbit Boy! Here, tie me up, too, cut me up! Be quick!" Iktome thought that he remembered Rabbit Boy's song. He thought there was much power in it—magic strength. But Iktome did not remember the words right. He sang:

> *Friends, friends,*
> *I have fought the moon,*
> *She tried to fight,*
> *But I won.*
> *Even battling the moon,*
> *I came out on top.*

They cut Iktome up, as he told them, but he never came to life again. The spider man had finally outsmarted himself. Evil tricksters always do.

Tatanka Iyotake's Dancing Horse

Told by George Eagle Elk

Some stories sound as if a person with a great imagination had invented them, but they are true. This is a true story that became a legend.

In the year 1890 the Ghost Dance came to the Sioux Nation. By dancing it and singing the right songs, the Lakota people thought they could bring back the good old times before the reservations, when the prairie was green and the buffalo plentiful, when nature was undefiled and the Sioux free to roam the endless plains on their fast horses. The Ghost Dance was peaceful, but the whites thought of it as the signal for a great Indian uprising. They asked for help from the army, and in the end many unarmed ghost dancers, mostly women and children, were killed at Wounded Knee. We Indians think that white people were afraid of the Ghost Dance because they had a bad conscience, having taken away half the remaining Indian land just a few

103

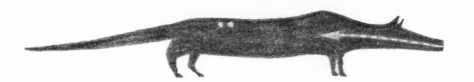

years before. People with bad consciences always live in fear—and they hate most those whom they have wronged. Thus it was with the Ghost Dance.

At the time Sitting Bull lived on the Standing Rock Reservation in North Dakota. He was not, as some people think, the war leader who had defeated Custer at the Little Bighorn. He was a holy man, the spiritual leader of his nation. He got along well with whites—some were his good friends—but he always said, "I want the white man beside me, not above me." Sitting Bull, or *Tatanka Iyotake* to call him by his Indian name, was a proud and dignified man, a good friend, but nobody's slave.

Now, at some time before 1890, Sitting Bull had joined Buffalo Bill's Wild West Show. He had traveled all over the country. In New York he could often be seen sitting at a doorstep on Broadway, giving nickels to poor street urchins and saying that

white folks did not know how to take care of their children. He also said that all children were alike in their innocence—red and white and black and yellow children—and that if only grown-ups could remain children in their hearts, all would be well. Sitting Bull and Buffalo Bill became friends. When the circus tour was over, Buffalo Bill Cody gave his friend Tatanka Iyotake a fine sombrero for a gift; the Indian holy man wore it from then on. Buffalo Bill also gave Sitting Bull his favorite circus horse. It was white and could do many tricks.

At that time the Great White Father in Washington, and the white agents who ruled the reservations, thought that the solution to what they called the "Indian problem" was for Indians to behave like whites, to speak and dress like whites, to become Christians and worship like whites, to own property and work like whites, to marry whites, and to be swallowed up by white society. The "problem" would be solved by simply having no more Indians, by putting them in the great American melting pot.

Sitting Bull opposed this. He did not want the Indians to die out. He wanted them to remain true to their old ways, to go on worshiping the Great Spirit, to continue speaking their own language and singing their native songs. And because Sitting Bull was a *wichasha wakan*, a medicine man, the most respected one among the Lakota people, many Indians rallied around him. Thus he became the center of the resistance to being swallowed up in the culture of the whites. Thus he also became the enemy of those who wanted to make Indians into white men.

They said that he stood in the path of progress. The Ghost Dance troubles seemed a good occasion to get rid of the old chief. He was accused of siding with the dancers and protecting them. The white reservation chief sent out the Indian police, forty-three of them, to arrest Sitting Bull. If he resisted and was

killed—so much the better. The police force was made up of what we now call "apples," men who are red outside and white inside, Indians who try to be like whites and who look down on their brothers and sisters as savages and heathens. These men think they are better because they wear the white man's uniforms and get his pay. The ones who were sent to arrest Sitting Bull were led by Lieutenants Shave Head and Bull Head.

They came to arrest the great leader in the predawn hours of an icy winter morning. The ground was covered with snow. They burst into his one-room log cabin with their six-shooters drawn. They dragged him naked from beneath his buffalo robe and pushed him outside; they would not even let him dress properly. They kept pushing him around as they put the handcuffs on him. The commotion woke Sitting Bull's friends and relations, who came boiling out of their tipis led by the old chief's friend and companion in arms, Chase-the-Bear. A woman's voice rose in a song:

Sitting Bull,
You were a warrior once,
What are you going to do now?

The old chief stopped abruptly. He pushed the policemen away, saying, "I won't go!"

Immediately one of the police chiefs shot him through the body, and an all-out fight to the death began. It is always said that a fight between Indians and whites is one thing, but when Sioux fights Sioux, watch out! The police tried to act like whites, but once the fight started, they became Indian warriors again. And among Sitting Bull's friends were some of the bravest men who had fought in many famous battles. When it was over, fifteen people lay dead or dying in the snow, among them Sitting Bull, Chase-the-Bear, and the police chiefs.

When the white horse heard the shooting, it thought it was back in the circus during the Wild West Show. It began dancing and prancing, sitting on its haunches and raising up its front legs, galloping in a circle, even rearing up on its hind legs, jumping around that way three or four times, bowing, curtseying, doing all the tricks it had been taught. In this way it honored its dead master in the only way it knew. All who saw it said that this horse was possessed, *wakan,* in the spirit way, and that this was proven by the fact that the horse was unhurt and untouched, though it had danced in the middle of a hail of bullets, right in the center of a crossfire. The white horse kept on dancing for a while after the fight was over and the bloody scene covered with silence.

Thus *Tatanka Iyotake,* the great Sitting Bull, holy man of the Lakota, and his favorite white horse became part of the legends of our people. Only their legend is true.

Iyan Hokshi, the Stone Boy

Told by Henry Crow Dog

When this earth was still young, there were ten brothers who lived together with their only sister, a beautiful girl just sixteen years old. She was all a young woman should be, at home on the prairie, well able to take care of herself and others, and good with her hands, especially in using porcupine quills to decorate rawhide dresses and leggings. There was much love and respect between the sister and her brothers. They took care of her, and she took care of them. They brought in the meat, she dug up *timpsila*—wild turnips—and gathered berries and nuts. They made the weapons necessary for their protection and for the hunt; she made almost everything else needed for life—a tipi of tanned hides, berry and nut pounders and grinders of stone, fleshers, scrapers, awls and needles of bone, shirts and moccasins of hide. In this way they lived happily. They had everything they wanted, and they had it because they made it themselves.

Every day the brothers would go out hunting while the girl was busy with her tasks in and around their camp. Every evening the brothers returned loaded with game—antelope one time, deer another. They would all sit together around the fire and relate to their sister what had happened while they were out after game. She, in turn, would tell them all that she had heard or seen at the campsite.

One night they came home as always, one after the other, all except the oldest brother. The brothers were not worried about him, thinking that he had simply strayed too far in pursuit of an elk or buffalo. But the sister had a strange and eerie feeling that something dreadful had happened. Her brothers tried to cheer her. "He is just holed up somewhere for the night," they told her. "Tomorrow he will be back." But she kept on worrying. At last the second oldest brother consoled her, saying, "I will go and look for him."

The next morning, eight of the brothers went hunting, but the second oldest went in search of his lost brother as he had promised. All the fears of the girl were confirmed. Not only did the oldest brother fail to show up, but the second oldest, too, was missing when the hunters returned. As you may already have guessed, the next day the third oldest went to find his two missing brothers while the other seven were hunting as usual, and as you may also have guessed, this time only seven came back and three brothers were missing. And so it went—all the young men vanished, one by one, until the young girl was left alone.

The sister was grief-stricken. She wept and the tears flowed down her lovely face, moistening her beautiful white buckskin dress. She went everywhere to look for her lost brothers, but could find no trace of them, not even a footprint. At last she sat down to think things out. "This is like a bad dream," she told herself, "but I am young and healthy and strong. I have learned to take care of myself. I will never give up hope that my brothers will return one day, and I will keep the campsite prepared for them."

109

The girl made herself a bow and arrow and hunted small game around the camp. She snared rabbits and quails. She gathered wild fruits and plants. She kept everything ready for her brothers, but they did not return.

One day, going about her daily chores to keep herself alive, the girl saw a round, odd-colored pebble on her path. It attracted her, and she picked it up. "This stone is *wakan*—enchanted," she thought. "I can feel it. This pebble has medicine power. I will put it in my sacred bundle. Maybe it will bring me luck." A little later she came to a small stream. She was loaded down with firewood, a basketful of chokecherries, and a sack of wild turnips. She needed her hands to steady her burden while crossing the brook. So she simply put the pebble in her mouth. But she stumbled and fell. The fall jarred her so that she swallowed the stone. In the days that followed, something very strange happened. The pebble inside her began to grow, and then to move. Finally she gave birth to a fine, healthy baby boy. And because he had formed himself out of the pebble—no ordinary pebble, to be sure —she named him *Iyan Hokshi*, stone boy.

She now grieved less for her brothers, happy to have a baby of her own to love. Iyan Hokshi grew fast, much faster than ordinary children. Almost from the moment of his birth he began to walk around. Quickly he learned to talk, and just as quickly he wanted to help his mother. He saw the bows of his lost uncles hanging in the lodge and reached for them. Small as he was, he already wanted to be a hunter. "These are too big for you, *hokshila*," said his mother. "Here, take mine." He took his mother's small bow and soon kept her cooking fire supplied with small game. Thus they lived together.

At last came the day when he asked his mother, "Whose bows are these hanging in the tipi?"

"They belong to your uncles."

"And where are these uncles of mine?"

She had to tell him then, though she was afraid of what he would do once he heard the whole story.

Her fears were realized because Iyan Hokshi said at once, "I must go and find my uncles."

"Wait. Do not leave me," she said and wept. "I never got over the loss of my brothers, but if I lose you, my only son, it will break my heart."

"Mother," he said, "do not cry. Keep that willow backrest ready for me in the tipi, because I will come back, and I will bring my uncles with me."

"How can this be? They were grown men, and you are only a boy. I know there is something dreadful waiting out there to destroy you as it has destroyed them."

"I am no ordinary boy. I am Iyan Hokshi the stone boy. I am afraid of nothing, and I will come back."

He took the biggest bow of his uncles, and a bagful of *wasna*—dried meat pounded together with berries—and his mother's medicine bundle. He went away confident, singing his song of war.

He wandered over the prairie, over hills, and through deep forests. He crossed rivers and mountains. He spoke to every animal he met, saying, "Do you know where my uncles are?" Sometimes he shouted as loud as he could. Once, someone shouted back at him, "Hrrn, Hrrrn!" It was a growling, ugly sound, the voice of a huge grizzly bear.

"Stop grunting, long face," said Iyan Hokshi.

"And you stop yelling. Who do you think you are talking to? You are disturbing my sleep. You better be careful how you talk to me, or you will be sorry."

"You are just a long-faced, red-eyed, puffed-up, loud-mouthed

nobody. Your breath stinks. Get out of my way!"

When he heard this insult, the angry bear attacked with tooth and claw, snarling and bellowing. But Iyan Hokshi made himself as hard as stone and as heavy as stone. He was like a rock, his skin like flint; and the enraged bear broke his teeth and claws attacking him. The bear soon was backing out of the fight, looking at Iyan with red, hateful eyes, saying, "You are not like other humans whom I have torn apart."

"I am Iyan Hokshi the stone boy, and I am afraid of nobody." He laughed at the bear. "Brother, you tickled me." And he walked on laughing.

As he was walking he heard the sound of *yamni-omni,* the whirlwind. Way up in the sky he saw a little speck, a black speck coming toward him which turned into a man, a giant. The giant put himself before Iyan Hokshi, saying, "Nobody can pass this way. I am no man to fool with. We will wrestle, and I shall crush you like an eggshell. Then I will throw you over that hill. Nobody has ever passed me."

Iyan Hokshi made himself heavy as stone and rock-hard and the giant could do nothing with him. Then Iyan Hokshi jumped up, bouncing against the giant. Iyan Hokshi was so stone-heavy that he broke the giant's ribs.

"You are not like the others," said the giant, holding his side.

"I am Iyan Hokshi the stone boy, and I am afraid of nothing."

Iyan Hokshi walked on. He entered a gloomy forest. He went deeper and deeper into it. He was aware that things changed as he went farther. It was very quiet. He could hear no sound, not even the call of a bird or the cry of a lone animal. It was

113

the silence of death. He came to evil-looking, fetid swamps which stank of sulphur and decay. But he marched boldly on. Poisonous, yellowish mists enshrouded him. They were icy and chilled him to the bone. Still he went on.

He noted that the forest itself was dead. All the trees had been killed by the poisonous air, making a forest of dead, dry stumps and branches, skeletons of trees covered with a hard, glinting yellow-white crust. Iyan Hokshi walked on. He came to a wide clearing in the forest, covered by swirling fogs. In the middle of this haze he made out the shape of a ghostlike tipi. Still he walked on. As he came nearer, he saw that the ground around the tipi was covered with whitened bones, the bones of men and animals. The huge tipi seemed to him as if it were made of human skin. He saw ten large bundles, the size of human beings, stacked upright against the tipi's side. "These must be my lost uncles," he thought. He entered the tipi.

Inside was an old hag. She was three times as big as an ordinary woman. Her teeth were like the fangs of a huge wolf, her eyes were the eyes of a snake. Her hands were like claws, and her long, white, matted hair reached to the ground.

"Welcome, welcome," she croaked, and a mighty croak it was. "It is not often that a nice, good-looking boy comes here. Sit down and eat." She had a fire going, and she stuck a few giant fistfuls of dry meat into it to roast. Iyan Hokshi did not like it, but ate it out of politeness. "Tomorrow we'll have something better," the woman cackled loudly. "Young, fresh, juicy meat." Her body shook with laughter.

She threw a ragged, moldy buffalo robe to Iyan Hokshi. "Here, sleep on this. This forest is dangerous at night. Better stay here." She fixed up a place for him to lie down. He only pretended to be sleeping, keeping a watch on her through half-closed lids. She noticed it. "Still awake?" she said. "In that case you might just as well come over here and do me a favor. I have a backache which is crippling me. Please rub my back."

He crawled over to her and massaged her back. Her body did not feel human. It was a monster's body. Her spine was as sharp as a knife's edge, and something was sticking out of it like a dagger, its point needle-sharp, like the curved fang of a giant rattlesnake. "It is probably poisoned," thought Iyan Hokshi. "This is how she killed my uncles."

"This rubbing is no good," said the old woman. "You are too small. You have no strength. Boy, get up on my back and walk up and down on it!" He did as she told him, carefully avoiding her spine and the sharp thing sticking out of it. He stomped on her a few times. She grunted, "Ah, that is better, but still not good enough. *Takoja*, grandson, jump as high as you can and as hard as you can, only that will help my backache."

Iyan Hokshi made himself as hard and as heavy as a rock. He jumped up as high as he could and came down on her like a boulder. It broke her back and killed her. Iyan Hokshi tossed the giant monster woman into the fire and burned her up. "I am Iyan Hokshi," he said, "and afraid of nobody." Then he went outside and opened the bundles one by one. In them he found the bodies of ten men—dry, cold, shriveled up, lifeless. He saw a few rocks strewn about the ground.

"Sacred rocks," he cried, "I am the stone boy. You brought me here. Tell me what to do." And the rocks told him. Iyan Hokshi put up a sweatlodge of willow sticks. It was the first

115

sweatlodge ever built. He covered it with buffalo skins from the monster woman's tipi. He put the ten bodies inside the sweatlodge in a circle. He made a fire and heated four times four rocks in it. On a forked stick he brought the red-hot stones into the sweatlodge. He closed the entrance flap so that no hot air could escape. He thanked the rocks and begged them once more to help him. He poured cold water over the hot stones from his skin bag, and immediately the little sweatlodge was filled with searing, white, purifying, life-giving steam. Iyan Hokshi began to sing and to speak. Four times he poured water over the rocks, begging them to use their power to bring these dead men back to life. As he did this for the fourth time, he thought he saw something moving through the clouds of white steam. He heard singing and talking. He opened the flap and let the steam escape. As soon as the air cleared and he could see again, he beheld ten young men sitting in the lodge, alive and well. These were his uncles, brought back from death by the power of the sacred rocks.

"This is what my mother wanted," said Iyan Hokshi. He brought his uncles back with him to his mother. You can imagine how happy she was.

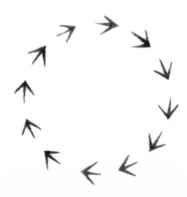

The White Buffalo Woman

Told by Lame Deer

One summer, untold lifetimes ago, the various bands of the Lakota Nation assembled for their yearly get-together. The land was beautiful, the prairie was covered with wildflowers, and the sun shone down on all—but there was no meat on the drying racks, nothing to eat but wild turnips, and the people were hungry. Among the tribes gathered were the *Itazipcho*, the Without Bows, and their chief sent out two young men to scout for buffalo.

These young hunters had to set out on foot because this was in the days before Indians had horses. It was a hard task to find game then. The two men searched a long time in vain. They did not even see the hoof print of a single buffalo. At last they came to the top of a hill from which they could see far and observe the whole prairie around them. Way off in the distance they saw a little speck moving, a tiny white dot coming toward them. They watched it getting bigger and bigger. At first they thought it was a buffalo, but it turned out to be a beautiful young woman, more beautiful than any they had ever seen before. A radiance seemed to envelop her.

117

She had on a dress of dazzlingly white buckskin so wonderfully decorated with quillwork that it made the young hunters wonder whether human hands could have fashioned it, or whether it was the work of spirits. The young woman wore her long blue-black hair loose, except for a strand on the left side which was tied together with buffalo hair. She wore a bundle on her back and carried a fan of sage leaves in her hand.

The young woman spoke to them. "I bring good things to your people. The Buffalo Nation sent me with a message to the Lakota Nation, a good message."

One of the two young men was so overcome by her beauty that he stretched out his hand to touch her, wanting to make love to her. But the woman was *lila wakan*, very sacred, and not to be treated in a disrespectful way. As soon as the brash hunter touched her, he was immediately struck by lightning, or as some wise old men tell the story, a cloud descended on him, hiding him from view. When it dissolved, all that was left of him was a heap of dry bones.

Now there was only one hunter left, a young man who treated the beautiful woman with the proper respect and admiration. She told him to go back to his people to prepare them for her coming. She told him what she wanted done. The people were to put up a large tipi with an *owanka wakan*—a sacred altar—inside it. She also wanted them to place a buffalo skull and a rack made of three sticks in the tent.

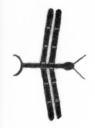

The young hunter returned to his village. He went to the chief and told him what had happened, and the chief told the *eyapaha*, the herald, to instruct the people. So this crier went round the camp circles calling out, "A woman, a sacred woman, is coming with a message from the Buffalo Nation. Receive her fittingly." The people put up the great tipi and did all things according to

the strange woman's wishes. At dawn of the next day all was ready. The herald once more made his rounds, commanding the people to gather in front of the tipi. There they stood waiting as the red ball of the sun rose over the horizon. They saw the beautiful woman approach in a sacred manner as if coming out of the rising sun. In her hands she carried the holy pipe. She was holding the stem with her right hand and the bowl with her left, and thus the pipe has been held ever since.

The woman entered the tipi where the old men of the tribe greeted her. "Sister, we are glad that you came. We have had no meat for some time, and all we can offer you is water." They dipped some *wacanga*, sweetgrass, into a skinbag of water and gave it to her this way, and to this day the people of the plains will dip sweetgrass or an eagle wing in water and sprinkle it on a person to be purified during a ceremony.

The White Buffalo Woman—by this name she has been known ever since—then showed the people how to use the pipe. She filled it with red willowbark tobacco. Then she walked around the altar, sunwise, circling from east to west. This represented the circle without end, the road of all life. The woman then placed a dry buffalo chip on the fire and lit the pipe with it. This was the fire without end, and the smoke rising from the bowl was as the breath of *Wakan Tanka*, the Great Spirit.

The White Buffalo Woman then showed the people how to pray with the pipe, lifting it up to the sky, up to the Grandfather, and down toward the earth, the Grandmother, and then to the four directions of the universe. "With this holy pipe you will walk like a living prayer," the White Buffalo Woman told the people, "your feet resting upon the earth, the pipestem reaching up all the way into the sky, your body forming a living bridge between the Sacred Beneath and the Sacred Above.

Wakan Tanka smiles upon us, because now we are as one—earth, sky, all living things, the four-legged, the winged ones, the trees, and the grasses together with the humans—now we are all one family, related to each other. This pipe is what holds us all together."

The White Buffalo Woman then addressed the women, telling them that it was the work of their hands and the fruit of their bodies which kept the people alive. "You are from Mother Earth," she told them. "Your task is as great as that of the hunters and warriors, your work as important as theirs." And therefore the sacred pipe is also something which binds men and women together in a circle of love. It is the one sacred object in the making of which both men and women have a hand. The men carve the bowl and make the stem, the women decorate it with ornamental bands of colored porcupine quills. When a man takes a wife they both hold the pipe at the same time, and red cloth is wound around their hands, thus tying them together for life.

The White Buffalo Woman then talked to the children, because they have an understanding beyond their years and also because, among the people of the plains, children are treated with the same consideration shown grown-ups. She told the little ones that all their fathers and mothers did was for them. That they, the children, were the most precious possession of the nation, that they represented the coming generations, the hope of the future, the circle without end. "Some day you will hold the pipe. Let it guide you always on the road of life. Grow up and then teach your children." This is what the White Buffalo Woman told them. The White Buffalo Woman then wrapped the pipe in its bundle and gave it to the Old Man Chief of the Itazipcho for safekeeping.

121

After she had done all this, the beautiful White Buffalo Woman took leave of the people, walking in the same direction from which she had come. As she was fading into the distance the people saw her turn into a white buffalo calf. It kept on walking until it disappeared over the horizon. Soon buffalo appeared in great herds, allowing themselves to be killed so that the people might live. And from that time on Brother Buffalo furnished the people with everything they needed—meat for their food, skins for their clothing and tipis, bones for their many tools. Thus the sacred pipe was given to the people. The Lakota people believe that this pipe still exists, somewhere on the Cheyenne River Reservation in South Dakota, kept by the descendants of the Itazipcho chief of old, to whom the White Buffalo Woman had given it many lifetimes ago.

The End of the World

Told by Jenny Leading Cloud

Somewhere, at a place where the prairie and the *Mako Sica*, the badlands, meet, there is a hidden cave. Not for many generations has anyone been able to find it. Even now, with so many cars and highways and tourists, no one has found this cave.

In the cave lives an old woman. She is so old that her face looks like a shriveled-up walnut. She is dressed in rawhide, the way people used to go around before the white people came to this country. She is sitting there—has been sitting there for a thousand years or more—working on a blanket strip for her buffalo robe. She is making that blanket strip out of dyed porcupine quills, the way our ancestors did before white traders brought glass beads to this turtle continent. Resting beside her, licking his paws, watching her all the time, is a *Shunka Sapa*, a huge black dog. His eyes never wander from the old woman whose teeth are worn flat, worn down to little stumps from using them to flatten numberless porcupine quills.

A few steps from where the old woman sits working on her blanket strip, a big fire is kept going. She lit this fire a thousand or more years ago and has kept it alive ever since. Over the fire hangs a big earthenware pot, the kind some Indian people used to make before the white man came with his kettles of iron. Inside the big pot, *wojapi* is boiling and bubbling. Wojapi is berry soup. It is good and sweet and red. That wojapi has been boiling in that pot for a long time, ever since the fire was lit.

Every now and then the old woman gets up to stir the wojapi in the huge earthenware pot. She is so old and feeble that it takes her a while to get up and hobble over to the fire. The moment the old woman's back is turned, the huge, black dog starts pulling out the porcupine quills from her blanket strip. This way, she never makes any progress, and her quillwork remains forever half finished. The Sioux people used to say that if the woman ever finished her blanket strip, in the very moment that she would thread the last porcupine quill to complete her design, the world would come to an end.

The Remaking of the World

Told by Leonard Crow Dog

You have heard enough Sioux stories now, so let me tell you one from another tribe. Up at Fort Belknap, Montana, live some people from the Gros Ventre tribe. One of them came and stayed with us for a while. He told us one of the ancient stories of his tribe, and as I remember it well, I will tell it to you.

There was a world before this world. The people in it did not know how to behave themselves or how to act human. The Creating Power was not pleased with this earlier world. He said to Himself, "I will make a new world." He had with Him the pipe bag and the chief pipe. He put it on the pipe rack made of three sticks in the manner of the Plains people. He took four dry buffalo chips. He placed three of them under the three sticks. The fourth one He saved to light the pipe. The Creating Power said to Himself, "I will sing three songs. They will bring a heavy rain. Then I will sing a fourth song and stamp four times on the earth with my foot. When I do this, the earth will crack wide open, and water will come out of the cracks. All the land will be covered by it." The Creating Power did all these things. When He sang the first song, it started to rain. When He sang the second song, it poured. When He sang the third song, the rain-swollen rivers overflowed their beds. But when He sang the fourth song and stamped on the earth, it split open in many places like a shattered gourd. Water began to flow from the cracks, covering all the land.

The Creating Power floated. He floated on the sacred pipe and on His huge pipe bag. He let Himself be carried by waves and wind, this way and that. He drifted for a long time. At last the rain stopped. All people and animals were drowned. Only *Kangi*, the crow, survived. It was flying above the pipe. It had no place to rest and was very tired. It cried out, *"Tunkashila,* Grandfather, I am very tired. I must soon rest." Three times the crow asked the Creating Power to make a place for it to alight.

The Creating Power thought, "It is time to unwrap the pipe and open the pipe bag." The wrapping and the pipe bag contained all manner of animals and birds. The Creating Power selected four animals known for their ability to stay for a long time under water. He first sang a song and took the loon out of the bag. He commanded the loon to dive and bring up a lump of mud. The loon did dive, but it brought up nothing. "I am exhausted," the loon said. "I almost died. I dived and dived but could not reach bottom. The water is too deep."

The Creating Power sang a second song and took the otter out of the bag. He ordered the otter to dive and bring up some mud. The sleek otter at once dove into the water, using its powerful, webbed foot to go down, down, down. It was under the water for a long time, but when it finally came to the surface, it brought nothing.

The Creating Power then took the beaver out of the pipe's wrapping. He sang the third song. He commanded the beaver to go down deep below the water and bring some mud. The beaver

thrust itself into the water, using its powerful, flat tail to propel itself downward. It stayed under the water longer than the others, but when it finally came up again, it brought nothing.

At last the Creating Power sang the fourth song and took the turtle out of the bag. The turtle is very powerful. Among all Plains Indians it represents long life and hardihood and the power to survive. A turtle heart is a great medicine. It keeps on beating for a long time after the turtle is dead. "You must bring the mud," the Creating Power told the turtle. The turtle dove into the water. It stayed below the surface so long that the other three animals shouted, "The turtle is dead. It will never come up again." All this time the crow was flying around, begging for a place to settle down.

After what seemed an eternity, the turtle broke the surface of the water and paddled to where the Creating Power floated. "I got to the bottom," the turtle cried. "I brought some earth." And, sure enough, its feet and claws, even the space in the crack on its side between its upper and lower shell, were filled with mud.

The Creating Power scooped some of this mud from the turtle's feet and sides. The Creating Power began to sing. All the time He sang, He shaped the mud in His hands, spreading it on the water, making a space of dry land for Himself. When He had sung the fourth song, there was enough land for the Creating Power and for the crow. "Come down and rest," said the Creating Power to the crow, and the bird was glad to do so. Then the Creating Power took from His bag two large wing feathers of the eagle. He waved these feathers over His plot of earth and commanded it to spread until it covered everything. Soon all the water was covered with earth.

"Water without earth is not good," the Creating Power

thought, "but land without water is not good either." He had pity on the land, and He wept for the earth and the creatures He would put upon it. The Creating Power's tears became oceans, streams, and lakes. "That is better," thought the Creating Power. Out of His pipe bag He took all manner of animals and birds and plants, and He scattered them over the land. When He stamped on the earth, all the animals came alive.

From the earth the Creating Power formed the shapes of men and women. He took red earth, and white earth, and black earth, and yellow earth to make human beings. He made as many as He thought would do for a start. He stamped on the earth, and the shapes came alive. They were the color of the earth out of which they were made. The Creating Power gave them understanding and speech, telling them what tribes they belonged to.

The Creating Power told the people, "The first world I made was bad. The creatures upon it were bad. So I burned it up. The second world I made was bad, too. So I drowned it. This is the third world I have made. Look, I have made a rainbow for you as a sign that there will be no more Great Flood. Whenever you see a rainbow, you will know that it has ceased to rain. Now, if you have learned how to behave like human beings and how to live in peace with each other and with the other living things in this universe, then all will be well. But if you make this world bad and ugly too, then I will destroy this world also. It is up to you."

The Creating Power gave the people the pipe. "Live by it," He told them. The Creating Power named the Western Hemisphere the Turtle Continent because it was there that the turtle came up with the mud out of which the third world was made. "Some day there might be a fourth world," the Creating Power thought. Then He rested.

129

Richard Erdoes, artist, photographer, and writer, was born in Vienna and has lived for thirty-five years in New York City with his wife, Jean. He made his first contact with the Indians of the Southwest over twenty-five years ago, as an outgrowth of a painting assignment on the scenery, people, and life of the Plains. Since then he has traveled innumerable times to Indian country, lived among the people there, and made many lasting friends. He and his wife now live part of the year in Santa Fe, where they have a small adobe house.

Very much involved with Indian affairs and the Indian Civil Rights Movement, Mr. Erdoes has written such outstanding and comprehensive accounts of Indian life as *The Sun Dance People* and most recently *The Rain Dance People*.

Paul Goble has felt the pull of the American Indian tradition "as long as I can remember," he says, "probably since the time my mother read me stories of Grey Owl and Ernest Thompson Seton"—and it was the wisdom of Black Elk which finally determined his life's orientation. Mr. Goble has made several trips to the United States, and each successive contact with the Indians deepened his insight into their ideas and ways. He was adopted into the Yakima and Sioux tribes, and given the name *Wakinyan Chikala*, Little Thunder, by Chief Edgar Red Cloud. He and his wife Dorothy are co-authors—and he the illustrator—of *The Friendly Wolf, Custer's Last Battle, The Fetterman Fight,* and *Lone Bull's Horse Raid.* Born in Haslemere, England, Mr. Goble now lives in London and teaches at Ravensbourne College of Art and Design.

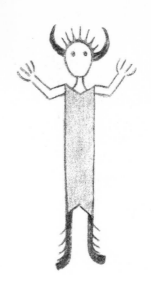

DATE DUE

The sound of flutes

Community Library
Sunbury, Ohio

1. Books may be kept two weeks and may be renewed once for the same period, except 7 day books and magazines.

2. A fine is charged for each day a book is not returned according to the above rule. No book will be issued to any person incurring such a fine until it has been paid.

3. All injuries to books beyond reasonable wear and all losses shall be made good to the satisfaction of the Librarian.

4. Each borrower is held responsible for all books charged on his card and for all fines accruing on the same.